A Memoir—Delivering Health Care in Cambodian Refugee Camps, 1979–1980

An American Nurse's Experiences that Launched Her into a Twenty-Five-Year Career in International Health

CHARLOTTE J. KNAUB

Copyright © 2014 Charlotte J. Knaub.

All rights reserved. No part of this book may be used or reproduced by any means, graphic, electronic, or mechanical, including photocopying, recording, taping or by any information storage retrieval system without the written permission of the publisher except in the case of brief quotations embodied in critical articles and reviews.

Balboa Press books may be ordered through booksellers or by contacting:

Balboa Press
A Division of Hay House
1663 Liberty Drive
Bloomington, IN 47403
www.balboapress.com
1 (877) 407-4847

Because of the dynamic nature of the Internet, any web addresses or links contained in this book may have changed since publication and may no longer be valid. The views expressed in this work are solely those of the author and do not necessarily reflect the views of the publisher, and the publisher hereby disclaims any responsibility for them.

The author of this book does not dispense medical advice or prescribe the use of any technique as a form of treatment for physical, emotional, or medical problems without the advice of a physician, either directly or indirectly. The intent of the author is only to offer information of a general nature to help you in your quest for emotional and spiritual well-being. In the event you use any of the information in this book for yourself, which is your constitutional right, the author and the publisher assume no responsibility for your actions.

Any people depicted in stock imagery provided by Thinkstock are models, and such images are being used for illustrative purposes only.
Certain stock imagery © Thinkstock.

Printed in the United States of America.

ISBN: 978-1-4525-1934-0 (sc)
ISBN: 978-1-4525-1936-4 (hc)
ISBN: 978-1-4525-1935-7 (e)

Library of Congress Control Number: 2014913488

Balboa Press rev. date: 09/18/2014

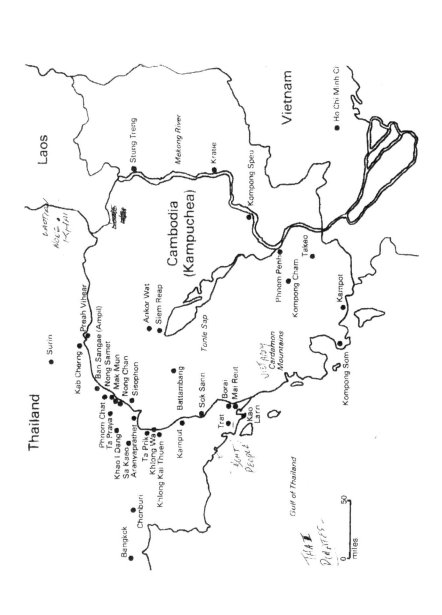

Contents

Who Is a Refugee?..ix
Foreword..xi
Preface xiii
Acknowledgement xvii
Introduction..xix
Cambodian Refugee Relief Experiences—1979-1980 xxi
    Country Background And Events....................................xxi
    November, 1979 The United States Response................xxiii

Chapter 1   On My Way, November, 1979 1
Chapter 2   Arrival In Thailand 3
Chapter 3   Sa Kaeo Camp And Aranyaprathet 7
Chapter 4   Urgent Needs Surveys..11
Chapter 5   Market Day With Suk Mei 15
Chapter 6   Countdown 18
Chapter 7   Extension!..22
Chapter 8   Immunization Program 25
Chapter 9   Family Planning 30
Chapter 10 Reasons To Stay?...34
Chapter 11 Live In The Here And Now..................................39
Chapter 12 Artie's Story- Do Adidas Make An
                 American Boy?... 44
Chapter 13 The Children-The Orphans, The
                 Unaccompanied Minors, And The Veterans 57

Chapter 14 Party-Party-Party! 62
Chapter 15 In The Merry Month Of May 66
Chapter 16 Trat And Mei Rut 71
Chapter 17 Bangkok--Refugee Status Conference 78
Chapter 18 Good-Bye Bangkok! Hello Nong Khai! 83
Chapter 19 Homecoming—Aran 92
Chapter 20 "The Star Trail" 95
Chapter 21 "Crisis Junky" 97
Chapter 22 Flying Tigers And International
            Organization For Migration 102
Chapter 23 Montana Is My Home 107
Chapter 24 Return And Countdown To Departure 111
Chapter 25 Sa Wa Dee, Thailand-Shalom, Israel 116
Chapter 26 Coming Home- December, 1980 121

Postscript 123
    Refugee Services Organizations
    Map of Camp and Holding Centers Locations in Thailand

Who Is a Refugee?

The formal, internationally recognized definition of a refugee is set out in the United Nations Convention relating to the Status of Refugees, which established the rights of people seeking asylum in a country other than their own, and the responsibilities of countries that grant asylum.

Approved at a United Nations conference in 1951 and brought into force in 1954, the convention initially sought to codify the rights of refugees in post-war Europe. In 1967, the convention was amended to include a protocol that broadened its geographical purview. There are currently 147 countries, including Canada, that have ratified the convention, protocol, or both.

Refugees are protected at a state level by humans rights legislation and national immigration and refugee laws, such as Canada's Immigration and Refugee Protection Act, and at international level by the U.N. convention, the United Nations High Commission for Refugees (UNHCR) and, indirectly, through various international covenants and charters guaranteeing human rights.

The pillar of the UN convention is the principle of non-refoulement. Meaning "to drive back", the French word, refouler, basically means that no refugee should be returned to a country where he or she is in danger of persecution.

The exact wording, as laid out in Article 33(1) of the 1951 convention is:

"No contracting state shall expel or return (refoul) a refugee in any manner whatsoever to the frontiers of territories where his life or freedom would be threatened on account of his race, religion, nationality, membership of a particular social group or political opinion."

Foreword

In "An American Nurse's Memoir of Personal Experiences in Thailand's Refugee Camps, 1979-1980, Charlotte Knaub provides a richly detailed accounting of the suffering, courage, and stamina of Thai, Laotian, and Vietnamese refugees in the aftermath of the Vietnamese War.

Whether one prefers fiction or non-fiction, Knaub's sensitive and often shocking depiction of her personal experience in war-torn lands takes the reader on a fascinating journey.

Filled with a courage and stamina of her own, Knaub's factual story is written, with both humor and pathos and is one that needs to be told, read, and re-read.

Joyce Lee McIntosh, PhD

Preface

This memoir is the personal account of my memories of my experiences and impressions in Thailand's camps for refugees and displaced persons in 1979 and 1980. In November, 1979, I was employed as an Infectious Disease Nursing Consultant with the Montana State Department of Health. I was offered the unique opportunity to join a team of epidemiologists to travel to Thailand. Our 90 day assignment was to administer communicable disease prevention immunizations to thousands of Cambodian children arriving in Thailand's refugee camps.

I had organized many immunization clinics in Montana's schools and communities. Recognizing that my limited international holiday travels in Canada, Mexico and South Korea hardly qualified me for this challenging assignment, I determined to at least learn more about the people to be in my care. Looking back, there was nothing that could have prepared me for the horrifying realty of the devastated men, women and children I met in the refugee camps.

A visit to the local library provided me with an overview of South East Asia, its people, their languages, and their customs but current information on Kampuchea was limited. From 1975 to early 1979, Cambodia endured a holocaust of unbelievable magnitude. After the Vietnamese overthrew the Pol Pot government, many Cambodians fled to the Thai border. The initial relief efforts took shape in the Thai border first-aid stations and later in newly established camps in Thailand.

On the cover of the November, 12, 1979 edition of TIME magazine, the headline reads "STARVATION, Deathwatch in Cambodia". There is a photo of a Cambodian woman holding an emaciated child. Inside the magazine are heart-rending images of exhausted mothers cradling hollow-eyed children with death's head faces, their bellies swollen, limbs as thin and fragile as dried twigs.

As a mother and a nurse, those images moved me to tears. I packed my suitcase and determined to travel to Thailand to help these people, especially the children. If polio vaccine, or vaccine injections could prevent any of these children from more suffering, or death, I wanted to help. Much later I realized that my decision offered me an opportunity to serve both in a crisis situation and to participate in an international response of management and cooperation in the largest refugee camp in the world.

Due to the constant turmoil associated with the arrival of thousands of refugees being transported to different camps, ninety days was not enough time to organize the vaccination clinics. My teammates from the Centers of Disease Control returned to the U.S. I negotiated an expansion to my contract and remained in Thailand for an additional 10 months, a decision I have never regretted.

During this time I had the opportunity to join together with people from around the world who came to relieve the suffering and meet the desperate needs of the Cambodian people. For most of the expatriates who participated in the relief operation and many of the Cambodians themselves, a sense of shared humanity was strongly experienced.

In writing this memoir, I focused on the relief activities in the holding centers inside Thailand, where I spent most of my time. Important emergency aid was also being rendered on the Thai-Cambodian borders and within Cambodia. The role of the United States, is emphasized, reflecting both the major part our country played in the relief operations and my more numerous contacts with the American relief community.

This memoir was started for my family, especially my eight grandchildren, to "tell the stories" behind the many photos, diary notes and artifacts I have collected. I wanted them to understand why I chose a nursing career, and the events that further propelled me into an international public health career that took me away from them for many years.

Studying my photos, re-reading my diaries and conversations with friends that shared those times brought back many memories of the events we had shared. The support and enthusiasm from members of The Sun City Center Writers Group, where I read my first chapters, further encouraged me to consider writing for publication.

An underlying purpose of the publication of this book is to motivate-and inspire- health professionals to participate in such activities in the future. To experience the challenges of assisting others to survive under seemingly impossible circumstances, to reach out to another human being, is what makes the difference between life and death, between hope and despair in a world where the multitudes of refugees continue to expand.

Acknowledgement

This book is in memory of the two million people who perished under the Khmer Rouge Regime. When their dying cries were at last heard, we had come to do what we could to relieve their plight.

This memoir would never have been written without the encouragement and clarification of dates and events by Dr. John Naponick and Dr. Amos Townsend, who were among the first people I met when I first arrived in Thailand in 1980. Our friendship has endured for more than 35 years.

Introduction

For the Cambodian people, whose history seems an endless succession of wars and occupations and suffering, 1975 marked the beginning of an era of terror unknown in previous times.

People would rather forget. The years of the United States involvement in South East Asia, the Viet Nam years, ended for most Americans in 1975.

Khmer Rouge soldiers overthrew the corrupt regime of Lon Nol. Literally, overnight, whole populations of Cambodian cities were moved to the countryside, under the ruse that America was going to bomb them. The Khmer Rouge tortured and starved the people. Deaths from diseases, malnutrition and execution were rampart; in what become known as the "killing fields."

When the horrors of Pol Pot and his regime were followed by the Vietnamese invasion, thousands of surviving Khmers, rather than live under the rule of their traditional enemies, fled, and crossed, Thailand's borders.

In 1979, Charlotte J. Knaub, is an Infectious Disease Nursing Consultant with the Montana State Department of Health. She was assigned to a team of epidemiologists from Centers of Disease Control who were traveling to Thailand. The 90 day contract was to organize clinics and administer disease prevention vaccines to thousands of Cambodian children arriving in Thailand's refugee camps. Those three months extended to thirteen months.

As she became aware that the relief operations reflected the unique opportunity for people around the world to join together in relieving the suffering and meeting the desperate needs of the Cambodian people, she determined to remain a part of it.

She compiled a "Public Health Nurse Resource Manual" for nurses working in Thailand's Refugee Camps, was published by World Concern, translated into six languages and used in many refugee camps.

She continued studies in international health through the University of Hawaii; administered maternal child health programs for refugees in Somalia, Macedonia, East Sudan, and Iraq. She served 10 years with World Health Organization, Western Pacific Region which encompasses projects in 32 countries. Although based in Manila, the author worked primarily in the South Pacific Islands of Papua New Guinea, Fiji, Kingdom of Tonga, Solomons Islands, Samoa, and Mainland China.

Cambodian Refugee Relief Experiences—1979-1980

Country Background And Events

Civilization in Cambodia began thousands of years ago. Its ancient temples reflect an advanced civilization with an intriguing culture and magnificent carvings and artworks. In the mid-19th century, Cambodia became a colony of France and remained so until 1953, when it won its independence. Prince Norodom Sihanouk was Chief of State and managed to maintain the nation's political neutrality among the superpowers. During the late 1960s, the Vietnam War increasingly encroached on Cambodian territory, including aerial bombing, causing death and destruction as well as political instability.

In 1970, the Sihanouk government was overthrown and replaced by Lon Nol's pro-western government. During the following five years, the forces of the Communist Khmer Rouge led by Pol Pot gained increasing power. In April 1975, the Khmer Rouge toppled the Lon Nol government. They renamed the country "Democratic Kampuchea" or the "People's Republic of Kampuchea." The five years of foreign interventions, bombardment and civil war ended. Thousands of Phnom Penh residents celebrated in the street as victorious Khmer Rouge troops entered the capitol. This joyous celebration occurred not because people supported the Khmer Rouge regime but because they felt relief that the five-year civil war had ended. They held the hope that Cambodia was finally at peace.

Embittered and toughened after years of brutal civil war and American bombings, the Khmer Rouge troops ordered the people to abandon their homes and leave the city, claiming "The Americans are going to bomb Phnom Penh!" There were no American plans to attack the city. The cities were emptied in an attempt to return the nation to a more primitive condition, free of "parasitic" foreign and modern elements. In the process, anything and anyone representing present-time civilization was destroyed. Schools were closed and books burned. Thousands of people died at the hands of the Khmer Rouge troops for such "crimes" as wearing eyeglasses or a wrist watch, symbols to the Khmer Rouge of Western civilization.

During the next four years, much of Cambodia was, in effect, a forced labor camp. In order to create the ideal communist society, all people would have to live and work in the countryside as peasants. Everyone-young and old, healthy and sick-was compelled to work, usually in the fields with primitive farming techniques. They had very little to eat, marginal housing and clothing, poor sanitation and virtually no medical or health-care services. Vaccinations for preventable diseases were banned.

Angka ("The Organization"), the secretive team of Khmer Rouge leaders, dictated the lives of every Cambodian citizen. Among the new rules, religion, money, and private ownership were all banned; communications with the outside world eliminated; family relationships dismantled. All previous rights and responsibilities were nullified. 2,000 years of Cambodian history had now come to an end; April 17 was the beginning of Year Zero for the new Cambodia: Democratic Kampuchea (DK).

From 1975 to late 1978, Cambodia endured a holocaust of unbelievable magnitude. After the Vietnamese overthrew the Pol Pot regime and installed a new government, people were free to leave the communes where they had been enslaved. Hundreds of thousands of starving, dispossessed, very ill refugees and the displaced Khmer Rouge troops fled to the Thai border in hope of finding refuge there.

November, 1979 The United States Response

The United States has long emotional ties with the countries of Indochina. Many Americans still have a strong personal involvement with and commitment to the Khmer. Americans are self-critical: some feel that although the United States fought to prevent the Khmer Rouge take-over, its policies may have contributed to their coming to power. Indirectly, the U.S. shared responsibility for what happened under the Khmer Rouge. In the minds of many at the U.S. Embassy in Thailand, in the late 1970's, was the feeling that the U.S. could have prevented the current events resulting in the massive influx of refugees.

Response of the U.S. Embassy by U.S. Ambassador Abramowitz, and people on his staff like Refugee Section Chief Lionel Rosenblatt, came quickly. The Ambassador's wife, Sheppie, was instrumental in motivating the American Women's Club in Bangkok to become personally involved in planning, organizing and delivering emergency humanitarian aid.

Other embassies in Bangkok, particularly the French, Swedish, Canadian and Australian, were seized with the enormity and severity of the situation, but only the United States Embassy sent personnel to directly work on emergency relief matters on the Thai-Cambodian border.

President Jimmy Carter appointed a group of highly qualified advisors, each with a special area of concern, to travel to Thailand and evaluate the crisis. This group included First Lady Rosalyn Carter, and Dr. William Foege, Director of the Centers for Disease Control in Atlanta, GA. Upon his return from Thailand, Dr. Foege requested a team of CDC epidemiologists to immediately travel to Thailand and implement vaccination programs for refugee children in Thailand's diseases, i.e. (DPT) diphtheria, pertussis, tetanus, polio and rubella.

Chapter 1

On My Way, November, 1979

When Dr. Martin Skinner, my current Bureau Chief with the Montana State Department of Health, and a former Centers for Disease Control epidemiologist, asked me if I'd be willing to travel to Thailand to assist with vaccinations of refugee children, I immediately said, "Of course! When do I leave?" In addition to infectious diseases investigations, my Nurse Epidemiologist position with the Bureau requires I organize and conduct vaccination clinics in schools throughout the state. I blindly assume the refugee program would be similarly organized. I could not have been more wrong---

My cross-cultural experiences are limited to Native Americans and Hispanic migrant workers. As a member of Montana's Friendship Force Exchange, I've traveled to South Korea, and frequently host guests from various countries. Recently, in Mexico City, I participated in an International Tuberculosis Congress, as this highly infectious disease is within the area of my responsibilities. Montana is a large state, requiring I spend 60% of my time traveling in-state. Additionally, I attend conferences in Atlanta, Denver, and Albuquerque one or more times annually. Constantly seeking opportunities to expand my professional education and experience in public health, I assure Dr. Skinner my passport and required vaccinations are current. I am prepared to leave. Nevertheless, I am startled when he announces, "That's good. Start your Fansidar (anti-malaria medication) today because you are leaving for Atlanta in 48 hours!"

While I have tentative support from my parents and sisters; my three young adult children are dismayed to find they will be on their own for three months. They are heartened with my assurances of additional income for their college expenses. The mountains surrounding Helena are already deep in snow as I depart Montana in a blinding snowstorm. In Atlanta, GA, I meet my four medical epidemiologist teammates from Centers for Disease Control. John, Brian, Richard, and Dale and I travel together to Washington, D.C. for a current refugee status orientation with the U.S. Department of State. This is not as informative as I anticipated and we depart for Thailand with sketchy knowledge of the conditions we will find, or detailed instructions of our assignment.

Our next stop is Heathrow Airport in foggy, chilly London but I stay warm in my spruce green parka. The long flight has given the team time to become better acquainted. I discover that this flight is the first time any of them have traveled out-of-country and dismayed to learn I am not only the oldest team member but also the more experienced in public health surveys and clinic organization.

None of these young doctors, fresh out of medical school, have conducted public health surveys or immunization clinics. I suspect Dr. Skinner was aware of this when he nominated me and had to assume I would be the "trainer" of these doctors. My previous experiences as "trainer of doctors" were less than successful. Nurses are generally resented for assuming to be more knowledgeable than a medical doctor, even if she or he is.

Chapter 2

Arrival In Thailand

Twenty eight hours after departing Washington, D.C., we arrive at Don Muang Airport, Bangkok, Thailand as the sun is rising. In moisture-laden, over-heated air, my spruce green parka is quickly discarded. Our schedule promises us three days in Bangkok for "recovery and duty orientation." Rueben, the U.S Embassy Field Officer who meets us, cheerfully informs us we would be driving directly to the Sa Kaeo Holding Center near Aranyapathet. He reports that the situation has worsened and we are needed at this camp, the first to open, now receiving 400-500 new refugees daily. Our hopes for a respite in an air-conditioned room, a warm meal and a refreshing bath quickly evaporate. It does not take long for me to become aware that a "change of plans" is the norm in these volatile situations.

The crisis is escalating at the Thai/Cambodian border. Mobile medical teams are urgently needed. Earlier in May, 40,000 Cambodian refugees had fled into southeastern Thailand but had been forcibly returned to their homeland by the Thai military. Many refugees had been found shot. Now, an estimated 50,000 refugees are massed at this border, and have begun pouring into the country. These desperate men, women, and children are extremely fearful, as they have no way of knowing if they will receive help or gunshots, or be turned back-again.

When I wearily step out of that cramped van eight hours later at Sa Kaeo Camp; in the dusty, oppressive heat of late afternoon, I can think of nothing but how differently I would imagine the look of a war zone. There are no gates, fences, or signs-just mud and bodies in an empty rice field, army tents and Red Cross flags; dust-laden air, a fierce sun and the fetid odor of sickness and death. Pieces of blue plastic, supplied by the United Nations High Commission for Refugees, hang on everything available, stretched out for covering, as far as I can see.

At the outset, the United Nations High Commission for Refugees (UNHCR) and the voluntary agencies were totally unprepared for the arrival of these refugees. Sa Kaeo Holding Centre, one of the first of 21 emergency shelters, had registered 31,000 Cambodians upon admission seven days ago. The daily death rate is an estimated 20-25.

For several months the fact of the signs and indications of a mass movement of refugees had been present; political maneuvering commenced but operational preparedness was minimal. Two thirds of the arriving volunteer, expatriate physicians and nurses are surgical or curative specialists when the greater needs are for preventive or public health approaches, i.e. latrines, sanitation, clean water, nutritional support and disease prevention through immunizations.

My personal "felt" needs and discomforts evaporate in the reality of the magnitude of misery surrounding me. My concerns of whether I eat or not, bathe, have a safe place for rest or not, are immediately made irrelevant. The team's original assignment and our plans for surveys and organized immunization clinics are also rendered irrelevant when I am immediately recruited to assist in triaging new arrivals. This process, a basic practice in disaster situations, provides an instant assessment of the sick and injured so the most appropriate care can be rendered more quickly. Rapid evaluation utilizes colored tags to indicate the degree of urgency for care and to which area they are to be taken.

GREEN TAG --- MINOR-WALKING WOUNDED.
YELLOW TAG --- DELAYED-SERIOUS, NOT LIFE-THREATENING
RED TAG --- IMMEDIATE-LIFE THREATENING INJURY
BLACK TAG --- MORGUE-NO PULSE OR RESPIRATIONS

It is very quiet. There is a sea of sick people all over the place crouching, squatting or lying on the muddy ground. The refugees are emaciated brown living carcasses, all limbs and eyes and folds of skin. Some shuffle around like zombies with glazed, expressionless eyes.

The last truck from the border unloads and we find the lifeless bodies of two young women and three, very small children, in a corner.

Unfortunately, too many are beyond our help, either dying or already dead. These receive the Black Tag and are moved aside while we concentrate on treating those refugees with Red Tags. Many are children, with the best chance for survival. Concentrating on performing tasks I had no previous experience in performing, I lose all track of time. Benumbed of body, mind and spirit, I sense, rather than feel, an arm around my shoulders, leading me away from the chaos. Several more arms lay me down on a lumpy mat and remove my mud-crusted shoes and splattered Levis. The prick of a needle in my left forearm and I slide into welcome oblivion.

Six hours later I awake to a cacophony of sounds and different languages and the odor of wood smoke and human wastes that would become familiar during my stay. My rescuers identify themselves as "The Best Emergency Response Team in the World!" This team of ten Israeli epidemiologists, led by Dr. Michaela Alkin, arrived at Sa Kaeo Camp at midnight, driving directly to the lantern lights in the Receiving Area. Experienced disaster medics, they have brought their own tents, food and water, as well as medical supplies. Recognizing my state of dehydration and exhaustion, they took care of me; rehydrating me with fluids, providing a rest area, clean "scrubs" and now a meal. During the following days I endure frequent teasing from this team as I am dubbed their First Refugee-the American lady that had to be rescued!

Chapter 3

Sa Kaeo Camp And Aranyaprathet

In the turmoil during our arrival at the refugee camp, I lose contact with Rueben and my teammates. Not having any other place to eat and sleep, I remain with the Israeli team. Michaela and Eli become my mentors, eager to orient me to disaster medicine and kosher foods. Within 48 hours we erect a 200 bed Infectious Diseases Ward, with 250 patients. Many family groups share the same platform-bed. All of our extremely thin, malnourished patients suffer from malaria, tuberculosis, dysentery, parasites and dehydration. I'm assigned to start intravenous fluids in their thread-like veins. Although I am out of practice, I quickly become more adept as I witness our patients revive with life-saving fluids and medications. Soon they are able to tolerate oral re-hydration fluids and food.

As the United Nations Camp Director has arrived with more aid workers and supplies, this holding center is becoming better organized while other sites are being prepared to open. I continue to work here for 10 days, curious as to the whereabouts of my Field Officer and teammates but too involved to worry. Are they, too, curious about my whereabouts, maybe even a bit concerned? Rueben finally appears and re-assures me he was aware that I was working with the Israeli Team, where my help was needed.

The others had decided that triage was not their 'assignment' so Rueben had transported them to a hotel in Aran. He now transports me to a designated house in Aranyaprathet where I am re-united with both my luggage and teammates. My male colleagues had stayed in the hotel, recovering from jet lag, heat, culture shock and unsafe food and water. The local beer was also sampled. They assumed I had moved into our assigned housing and was working in the newest holding center-Khao-I-Dang.

Rueben informs us our team has been seconded to the United Nations High Commission for Refugees. Our revised assignment: "to conduct surveys to determine general health status in Sa Kaeo and twelve, newly opened Cambodian, Vietnamese, and Laotian holding centers and camps in regards to environmental conditions, food rations availability and quality of health care services." Again, the recognized common denominator is the absence and inadequacy of disease prevention and health promotion programs.

We am dumb- founded to learn that little planning is being given to erect suitable and adequate latrines, the provision of sufficient water tanks for the increasing numbers of refugees, or even sprayers and supplies for insect control. Priority is given to erecting surgeries and 200 bed specialized treatment centers, hence the urgency to staff them with surgeons, internists and clinical nurses.

Our base is in Aranyaprathet, a small, Thai village about ten miles from the Cambodian border. Our team is assigned lodgings in an eight room house. This house belongs to a large, local Thai family and has been built entirely by their own hands. All nine members of the family have moved to bamboo and grass-thatched huts behind their home. Our agency has employed them as cooks, housekeepers, guards, drivers, translators and resident seamstresses and barbers. Initially, this situation was uncomfortable for me as I didn't understand why this family so willingly gave up their spacious home to the farangis. As I become acquainted with the family, and a close friend of the owner's wife, Suk Mei, I come to better understand the various financial and educational benefits of this arrangement for this family.

The home is built in typical Thai style, elevated one story up, with the lower area entirely encased in metal fencing and used for storage of our medical supplies. There are four verandas, one on each side of the house and each with a distinctive purpose. The main entry veranda, reached by an expansive set of stairs, is for arrivals, departures, and lounging. The other verandas are for cooking, dining, and bathing. The interior is an "open" design with dividers rather than walls.

The floors are made of hand-hewn teak wood and shoes are always removed before entering. With the family's furniture and personal belongings removed, 17 cots, swathed in mosquito netting, are grouped randomly throughout the house. Initially I am dismayed at the obvious lack of privacy but soon find that this "lack" is of minor consequence as more serious concerns are presented. Our sponsoring organization, International Refugee Committee, places all their volunteers here, where their terms of service may be as brief as thirty days or as long as a year. The volunteers- doctors, nurses and medical students, come from hospitals all over America. There is a constant turn-over of housemates but usually 24 or more men and women are "in residence" at any given time. Most of us work in the daytime, and some of the volunteers rotate to the Thai border camps for 24 hour duty. Others might stay in Sa Kaeo or Khao-l-Dang hospitals for night duty. It becomes interesting when an occasional overflow requires a "doubling up" of new best friends

Accustomed to a more conventional life style, I arrange a relatively private space and gain assurances from our landlady, Suk Mai, no one else would be allowed to sleep in my cot. Several of the volunteers were closer in age to my own sons and daughter, so I "pulled rank". Claiming my age (46) and experience give me seniority, I am awarded with more privacy from my housemates amid humorous references to my "state of decrepitude".

The open-air "bathing veranda" is at the back of the house. Watching the ferangis perform the challenging bathing ritual has quickly become a daily entertainment event for the villagers. It goes like this. Wearing a sarong tied under my arms, I stand in a pink plastic basin and dip water from a waist high clay jug, which I pour over my head and shoulders. Then I soap, and rinse. Next, I crouch over the basin and wash my legs and thighs as far up as possible. By now my sarong is dripping wet, so I step out of the basin, and pull a dry sarong over my shoulders while I shimmy out of the wet one. I step back in the basin to wash my feet. Water is a precious commodity so I learn to leave my bathwater that will be used to scrub the steps. The villagers keep silent throughout my bath but then start talking and laughing as soon as I finish. This does not happen when the men bathe, only when any of the women bathe.

Our single bathroom is typical Asian design: a small window for light in a narrow space with a squat commode, a water jug with a dipper, and a constantly wet, tiled floor with a short plastic shower curtain in the doorway. Tissue is optimal. This commode also has a large, noisy, resident bullfrog that leaps out of the commode and through my legs, as soon as I am in "crouch" position. This is one of the times I envy the males their better designed apparatus as they can remain standing while being greeted by Mr. Bullfrog.

Chapter 4

Urgent Needs Surveys

For two weeks the team conducts the assigned surveys from our base in Aran. On the road by 6:00 A.M., we take advantage of the cooler, morning air. Our Thai driver, capable, but with limited English- speaking skills, keeps a sharp-edged 36 inch machete at his side. We plan to finish the surveys of 7 camps, 2 older ones and 5 new ones, as quickly as possible so we can start the children's vaccination program before there is are any outbreaks of preventable diseases, i.e. measles, pertussis, diphtheria, and polio. Additionally, we also locate three, small older camps, that were not on our list, with 30-60 Chinese and Viet Namese displaced persons in each.

We encounter numerous delays due to bad roads, poor directions, misinformation and numerous security check-points. Although we, our driver, the van and our supplies have the required permits to travel in designated areas, the armed militia doesn't always recognize, or accept, them. We present our passports on demand and suffer real consternation when they disappear from sight and do not re-appear quickly. When we are identified as medics, "American medicines" are often requested. An offering of payment may be interpreted as an attempt to bribe the guard, and we are turned back. Other times we are requested to "declare and show" how much money we are carrying. We have to trust our driver for the translations and negotiations. It takes several attempts to obtain entry to three of these newer camps.

These camps, within sight of the Cambodian border are fenced and guarded. The local Thai villagers gather to watch us we arrive and depart. They are very poor, living in extreme hardship, and lack basic health care, schools, clean water and sanitation services. Now they must witness thousands of refugees provided with these services, free of charge or labor. I wish to understand more about this situation and make a mental note to discuss this situation with Suk Mai, my Thai landlady.

All our food and water supplies for the day must be carried with us. Without an ice cooler (no ice!) we drink bottled, safe, but warm water, without complaint. My colleagues usually eat their food supplies of fruit and bread by mid-morning so we are on a constant look-out for markets and food stalls. In these rural areas there are no restaurants, only small stalls and street vendors selling fruits and vegetables, soup, rice, steamed dumplings and chicken- on-a stick-satay.

I watch the re-used plastic tableware being washed in greasy, dirty water and shudder. At all times I carry my Montana camp kit, supplemented with new chopsticks, so have my boiling hot, spicy soup ladled into MY clean cup. It is extremely hot and humid and the soup makes me perspire even more profusely. Hopefully I decide there must be some healthy benefit to always being damp and sticky besides attracting mosquitoes. Fresh "finger bananas", mandarins, lychees, and rambutans are plentiful and provide rehydration and vitamins. Their skins are easily removed making them safe to eat. The spicy soup also makes me thirstier so I drink more water which leads to a search for a latrine, or very tall bush!

Our team attracts attention wherever we go, but wherever I am small groups of villagers gather to observe my every movement. Visitors to these rural areas are few, very rarely American, and never a red-headed, freckle- skinned woman. I have yet to meet anyone in these villages who speaks any English and my own progress in learning Thai is dismal. I yearn to be able to communicate with the villagers to learn what their feelings are in regards to the influx of foreigners—refugees and aid workers. I am becoming accustomed to being constantly watched and am learning to simply accept the unwanted attention. The loud chatter doesn't disturb me as much as the silence that often falls when I appear; and starts up again as I depart.

Our initial "urgent needs" surveys are finally completed. We are at our Aran house, collating our findings and detailing an action plan to start the immunization clinics in the camps. More refugees are arriving daily in the newest camps with an estimate of 50,000 now in Sa Kaeo and 150,000 in Khao Dang. We are in the sixth week of our 12 week commitment and I'm feeling more and more "urgent" myself; concerned we will be unable to fulfill our assignment to vaccinate the children.

Thousands of doses of donated vaccines are stored in refrigerators in a large, metal, warehouse; 15 kilometers from Sa Kaeo, and 25 kilometers from Khao-I- Dang. Transporting thousands of doses of vaccines requiring refrigeration, and maintaining the required temperature once we arrive at the camps will be our first challenge. Without electricity, we will have to depend on oversized coolers and ice packs. We plan to arrive as early as possible, during cooler morning hours, and administer vaccines for 3 hours. This is the maximum time we estimate our ice supply will maintain the required temperature to safeguard our vaccines effectiveness.

The vaccines will be administered via jet guns; each gun holding 25 dose vials. With 20 jet guns in use, (and 4 in reserve); we estimate 3,000 doses of DPT can be delivered each day, along with oral polio vaccine, to children under age 7 years. At this rate, we estimate we need 21 consecutive days to administer 23,000 doses; and within the following week, start the second round.

Spending these two days "off road" is restful and allows me to catch up on my laundry and mail. It takes two weeks for mail to travel from Montana to our Bangkok headquarters, and often an additional 10-14 days to reach me in Aran. In this latest bundle I have many letters from my family, friends and colleagues. I can't imagine what their motive is in assailing me with descriptions of numerous meals prepared and eaten. My sister, in response to my description of the local toilet tissue as sandpaper grade #3, offers to ship rolls of Charmin's softest products!

I feel a distance developing that has less to do with the thousands of miles that separate us, and more to do with the changes in my own lifestyle and activities. Witnessing the tragedies in the lives around me, I am beginning to feel that three months will not be long enough to accomplish my assignment. Further, I am doubtful that team replacements, if any, will be prepared to tackle the enormous challenges of vaccinating an estimated 50,000 children. More children arrive daily and these newest arrivals appear even more ill and malnourished.

Chapter 5

Market Day With Suk Mei

Suk Mei, my landlady and friend, decides I need to "go to market" with her and I eagerly climb on the back of her new motorcycle. The entire family now ride new motorcycles and rarely are seen walking anywhere, as they did when I first arrived. Our first stop is the local beauty salon; a one room thatched hut with bamboo mats covering the dirt floor. Electrical cords are looped around the center post to connect to a small fan, the hair dryer and the curling wand I have been requested to bring with me. There are two small chairs, several buckets of water, plastic basins, pitchers, and a stack of small towels, but no hairdresser. Suk Mei and I perch on small three-legged stools and -wait and -wait and -wait.

I ask Suk Mei, "Do we have an appointment?" She looks blankly at me but stands up, laughing and shouting loudly out the doorway. Three giggling young ladies, carrying plastic basins of clippers and combs, crowd into the small room. They are brightly dressed in jewel- colored silk sarongs and wear heavy make-up. Their thick, jet black glossy hair is arranged in formal styles, similar to the Queen's. I am their first American customer and they have dressed for the occasion. Compared to these lovely girls, I feel quite aged.

My feet are placed in a basin of water and Lovely Girl #1 proceeds to vigorously scrub them and my legs with a white piece of rough soapstone. Lovely Girl #2 puts my hands in another basin of water and massages my neck and shoulders. After an hour of cleaning, massage, and oiling, Lovely Girl # 3, who had been occupied with styling Suk Mei's long hair, turns to me and indicates it is my turn to be "styled". With gestures and pantomime, I indicate that I wish to have my thick, shoulder length hair cut short as I've decided less hair would be easier to maintain. All four ladies loudly protest but I insist, though inwardly fearful of what the outcome will be.

By this time, various aged small children come and depart, happily playing among the cords and feet. Various faces appeared in the doorway and in the open spaces between roof and walls. They seem to be asking questions of my beauticians, who give long responses overlaid with bursts of giggles. All three ladies are parting and clipping my hair so I close my eyes and think "mai pen rai" (what will be, will be).

It is finished. There is lots of my rust-colored hair on the floor which is quickly swept up. I learn later that small swatches were sold. The on-lookers melt away and since there is no mirror in this establishment, I'll have to wait until I get home to view the results.

Suk Mei remains silent as we climb on her "moto" and head for the fresh market. This market is "open air", under a large awning, with produce piled everywhere. The dirt floor is ankle-deep in garbage and covered with flies. Items for purchase have no prices as customers must "haggle" with the seller. Suk Mei is very good at this as the point is to leave both seller and buyer satisfied, with neither one feeling cheated. We purchase various fruits and vegetables in this manner and proceed to the fresh meat and poultry section. There is no refrigeration. Whole sections of beef are hung from a low rafter and when the buyer indicates which "piece" they wish to buy, haggling begins. The selected "piece" is sliced off, and wrapped in a banana leaf. The poultry—chickens, ducks, and geese---are kept alive until purchased. They are hanging by one leg on a rope, flapping their wings and squawking loudly. We can take our purchase home alive or the seller will twist the head off of our purchase-free of charge! After this adventure I determine to convert to an all- vegetarian and rice diet.

Our "moto" is heavily loaded with me and the produce but we arrive home without incident. I immediately head for the mirror in the washroom to view my new hair-do. Wow! What a difference a good haircut can make! I hadn't been aware of losing weight and acquiring a tan but have done so and actually look much younger with the boyish haircut.

Chapter 6

Countdown

Time is flying by rapidly and I'm increasingly anxious. I try to focus on our team's main objective: to organize and implement vaccination programs. My team mates are more focused on sight-seeing and 'farangi' parties than in program planning. My nagging suspicions of their collective disinterest is confirmed when Brian spoke for them all. "We are doctors but none of us have ever actually planned or conducted mass immunization clinics. We have been working as epidemiologists with specific roles in already-functioning systems. You've had more actual public health field experience than all four of us combined but you can't do it alone. Someone else will have to start the clinics after we leave."

As a result of the efforts of Dr. Foege, we are among the first American epidemiologists to have arrived in Thailand early in the relief operations. Our assignments and roles had not been defined but clearly required innovative approaches and adaptation to 'what is---not what we wished it were". Dale admits he feels totally overwhelmed and depressed, is anxious to return to the U.S., and the others agree. I was glad to finally have an open discussion with these young men, fresh out of medical school, and with little real life or professional experience. It is regretful we didn't have it sooner.

A Memoir—Delivering Health Care in Cambodian Refugee Camps, 1979–1980

It appears that we will have accomplished very little of our assignment before our departure, scheduled for less than one month away. Are these months going to be a waste of time and money? I hate to think that I came here and then left without contributing more to relieve the misery of the helpless refugees. I think of the fate of the children who have survived against all odds to come this far, only to unnecessarily suffer, or die, of measles-or whooping cough-or polio-or tetanus.

The jet guns are here, in a carton, under the house. The vaccines are under refrigeration 5 kilometers away. I am here-- and it is time for me to decide to leave as scheduled-- or remain. To remain, I require permission from my Bureau Chief in Montana, and a Visa Extension and a Work Permit from the Thai authorities, which requires a sponsor or an agency contract. As much as I would like to, I cannot volunteer as I need income to support my own family. My children are expecting me home soon. They were dubious about this 'adventure' in the beginning; I doubt if they would understand my decision to remain longer in Thailand. Where do I begin?

I start with Vit, a relative of our landlord who is always available. Vit is one of the 37 people now living within our compound. He is indispensable as our driver, translator, guard and source of gossip and information. He is about the age of my second son, and convinced that I am a "movie star, maybe like Shirley McLane". I suspect that Suk Mai has arranged this "job" for him as she has often expressed her wish that I stay longer and not leave "too soon." Vit readily answers my questions about where important people can be found, but it is Suk Mai who transports me on her moto to the UNHCR and ICRC offices on the outskirts of Aranyaprathet.

Their offices are side-by-side and I am fortunate to arrive during a large meeting. It is assumed that I am the American team representative for Centers for Disease Control and I leave it at that. I am introduced to ICRC Coordinator, Magnus Grabe, Dr. Don Allegra and Dr. Phillip Nieburg, CDC epidemiologists who are "on loan" to the ICRC.

The purpose of this meeting is an initial attempt to identify and register all voluntary, private, religious, local and international groups who are providing aid to refugees in S.E. Thailand. It is estimated that at least 80 (ATTACHMENT LIST-A) groups are working in this area. There is also an unknown number of private individuals, resulting in duplications of services in some areas while other areas are under-served. These private individuals have arrived from all corners of the world, speaking multiple languages, and with differing attitudes and standards of care. Humanitarian relief for the refugees is the purpose and the ultimate motive for each endeavor, but sometimes purely ambitious, political, evangelistic, or other aims take precedence. Competition among the volags is evident as they vie to 'register' the highest number of patients under their care.

Following the meeting, I meet with Magnus, Don and Phillip, to explain the original purpose of my visit: to acquire another contract in order to conduct the immunization programs. My request is received with enthusiasm, and I find that that they, like I, have been working without specific guidelines from previous refugee experiences. Magnus will obtain the required documents for me to remain until 30 April, 1980, under a contract with International Rescue Committee. We all agree that the immunization program is our top priority and must be started as soon as possible in Khao-I-Dang and Sa Kaeo camps.

Within the following week, I meet with Dr. Daniel Susott, Khao-I-Dang Medical Co-ordinator, who has been organizing public health activities within the camp. Daniel speaks French and has been rapidly learning both Thai and Khmer, definite assets when a translator is unavailable. He has identified many educated and skilled refugees-doctors, nurses, lab technicians, and teachers who had not been able to practice their professions under the Khmer Rouge but are willing to help us. Daniel and I meet with Khmer section leaders to organize a reporting system whereas we are quickly alerted to new cases of suspected communicable diseases.

Chapter 7

Extension!

There is so much to do in a very short time. We've scheduled the first clinics to start in two weeks. I've only been away from my "real life" in Montana for 8 weeks but it feels like years. This new "real life" is much more exciting and challenging than the old one, but first I must have conversations with my family, and my Bureau Chief.

As my teammates are scheduled to depart within a few days, Vit drives us the five hour trip into Bangkok, that very busy, noisy and modern city. The contrast between 'the city' and 'the countryside' spans a hundred years and overwhelms me.

We stay in the very posh President's Hotel, enjoying air-conditioned comfort, and marveling at the flush toilets. I indulge myself with a two hour, hot water soak in a real bathtub. When we visit the dining rooms, the expansive array and variety of foods on the buffet tables overwhelm me and I find I have little appetite for the rich foods and the huge slabs of fatty meats and rich desserts. I think, "Five hundred refugees could have been fed from these tables alone." My soon-to-be-former teammates join the diners but when I notice many servings of uneaten foods being wasted, I leave the dining area in disgust. Why don't more people care about those thousands of starving children massed in the camps and on the borders, a mere five hours away? Do they not have a conscience?

A Memoir—Delivering Health Care in Cambodian Refugee Camps, 1979–1980

At the U.S. Embassy, I complete the required paperwork and am relieved to be assured I am a "Legal Guest Worker" for at least another three months. While here I have an opportunity to meet Sheppie Abramowitz, the U.S. Ambassador's wife. She is instrumental in organizing women's groups to collect and deliver food and clothing to refugees on the border. I am introduced to several of these volunteers who ask me many questions about the particular needs of the children. Sheppie informs me that she will be accompanying Mrs. Rosalyn Carter, who will be soon visiting the camps on a fact-finding mission for President Jimmy Carter. She promises to try to locate me during the visit so I might speak with their group. I am so excited and happy that I decided to stay! Not only am I actually enjoying my work with the refugees but have opportunities to meet many interesting people.

I procrastinate, and am running out of time as I must return to Aran soon. At the International Refugee Committee Office I send a TELEX to Dr. Skinner, the Montana State Health Bureau Chief, and to Dr. Anderson, Director of Montana State Health Services, informing them of the refugee situation, the surveys, plans to start the clinics---- and my three month extension.

My three children live in three different places in Montana. I figure out the 12 hour time difference and as I dial the many numerals needed to connect us, I try to predict their reactions. Each seems stunned that I am able to call from "so far away", and have difficulty understanding our conversation. Scott, my oldest son, simply says "O.K. So, when will you come home?" My daughter, Laurie, starts to cry, says she misses me a lot, and "when will you come home?" My youngest son, J.C., is hurt, becomes angry, and hangs up before I have a chance to explain my decision. I am happy to hear their voices but really not surprised with their reactions. I think this separation, although painful now, will be beneficial for them as they learn to become more responsible for themselves. Time will tell------

In the event I was unable to talk to my children directly via telephone, I have written long letters, hoping for their understanding. I add notes of love and appreciation and post them. I realize that they are unable to comprehend how much it means to me to finally be able to make my own decisions at this time of my life. This is the first time I have ever been actually on my own, with the freedom to decide how I want to live and work, to choose my own friends, and explore –and learn—and—and—OH—there is so much I want to do!

Chapter 8

Immunization Program

Upon completion of the UNHCR surveys, which provide estimates of the 'probable' numbers of under-5 year olds, I was assigned Team Leader for Khao-I-Dang Camp, with Dr. Don Allegra, Epidemiologist, as my consultant. Don also was responsible for the other 23 camps, as well as the border First Aid stations. Working with Don is a privilege as he challenges me constantly with questions, and is always teaching, both I and our Khmer helpers.

Khao-I-Dang is the largest holding center, located in a rice paddy that measures about 4 square miles. It is the second largest aggregation of Cambodians in the world, the second largest "city" in Thailand, and twice the population of the largest city in Montana. K-I-D was closed to new arrivals when the population reached 140,000, but 800 newborns are hospital-delivered each month, with unknown numbers of "hut deliveries".

The children, constituting over 20% of the population, are the focus of my attention. I am overwhelmed by their sheer numbers and admire their tremendous tenacity to cling to life, persisting in surviving with all the odds against them. They deserve all the assistance we can offer in their struggle to survive. Vaccinating as many as possible against preventable diseases became our major goal.

Over-vaccination is not a concern as it is well known that Pol Pot had discontinued most medical programs. There have been no immunological vaccines available in Kampuchea for at least five years. Older children are also at risk but hopefully have some protection from previous programs, IF there are no outbreaks of preventable diseases.

One of our many concerns, though, is the compromised condition of the children. Malnutrition is evident in every child. Malaria, tuberculosis, parasites, respiratory and diarrheal diseases are common. Will there be adverse effects from the vaccines due to their physical weaknesses? We won't know until we vaccinate.

The obstacles to conducting mass vaccination clinics in the camp are numerous. Within the camp I have many Khmer helpers. Doctors, nurses, pharmacists, lab technicians and medical students have volunteered. One such student, Yat Nei, became my chief translator/record keeper, and close friend.

These young people had not been allowed to study or work during the Khmer Rouge regime but are anxious to help wherever they could. Six teams are organized and trained to sort, register, administer, translate, explain and encourage. They work long hours in the heat, not merely for the extra food rations that we are allowed to "pay" them, but out of pride and a desire to contribute to their community. Twelve young males are trained to operate the jet guns to rapidly inject multiple doses of vaccine. They have never seen these guns before, nevertheless, their enthusiasm overrides their lack of ability and with practice, quickly become adept.

Outside the camp, I have sole responsibility for the organization of vaccines, supplies and transport. Dr. John Naponick, Medical Coordinator for all the vo-lags, and now living in the same house as I, helped me whenever he could. Sustaining the cold chain to ensure live-virus vaccine potency, organizing the daily collection of vaccines, jet guns, ice coolers, supplies and transportation, and passing border control checks—became a daily routine for the 21 day cycle required to complete each campaign. Each day our supplies had to be carried in and out of the camp. Each of the 24 jet guns used in administering the vaccines required cleaning and testing at the end of each day. I entrusted this chore to no one but myself. Supplies had to be replenished from our storage crates in the wired enclosure under the house and the ice supply assured.

All vaccines are sensitive to heat to some extent, and especially the freeze-dried vaccines. Our vaccine supply is stored in refrigerators and a freezer in a near-by warehouse. These units are electric, and in the event of a power failure, not infrequent here, back-up generators are connected. There are guards on duty 24 hours a day. In the middle of our measles vaccination campaign, the power did fail. The guards were unable to immediately start the back-up generators and our vaccines were left in a non-cooling unit for an unknown length of time.

Do we continue to use this vaccine, with unknown effectiveness? This would give false assurance to families, who are already dubious of our Western medicine's ability to prevent diseases. My colleagues, contending that partial protection might be rendered, disagreed with my decision to not use this vaccine. I suspended the clinics and forwarded vaccine samples to a Bangkok lab for testing. Seven days later the results of the tests arrived with a fresh shipment of vaccine. The vaccine is not viable and would not have provided any protection.

Perhaps because of these many obstacles, conducting the clinics becomes a personal challenge for me. Although thousands of children are vaccinated, it seems as if we will never get ahead of the epidemics. The initial outbreak was rubella (measles) and a special 200-bed ward was opened for the many cases with complications. Mortality was high due to the compromised status of the children, and did not decline for over six weeks after the start of the campaign. DPT (diphtheria-pertussis-tetanus) immunizations were scheduled but delayed due to reports of polio cases in the border camps. We give initial oral polio doses to as many children as possible, fully aware that three doses are required to prevent the disease. One dose is better than none. Hopefully, we can complete the series before the children move on-or out, or die.

Due to the constant mobility of the refugee population and unreliable record-keeping, it is impossible to determine the rate of protection actually obtained. We make every attempt to vaccinate each child with the required series of three of each vaccine. I witness the agonizing deaths of two male youths from tetanus (lockjaw), and cry at the loss. Typhoid and cholera epidemics threaten but are contained with rapid recognition and action from the K-I-D-Khmer Public Health Department

A small but increasing number of reported cases and deaths from meningococcal disease are reported. Vaccine is donated by an American pharmaceutical company. 20,000 young adults are vaccinated by the Khmer Vaccination Team; who had become quite adept with the jet guns.

It takes months but the general health of the children show improvement. A first week, a second, and a third week pass without reports of new outbreaks of preventable diseases. The need for mass clinics—the urgency, the early awakenings and endless days, the headaches dealing with obstacles and breakdowns, the continual anxiety about the quality and quantity of vaccines was over, as were the unnecessary deaths.

CDC Epidemiologist, Dr. John Horton, our long-anticipated replacement, arrives. He is welcome but I resent his presence now that the crisis situation is under control. Six weeks ago, when exhaustion threatened to overwhelm me, his help would have been even more welcome. The immunization program is the reason I came and the reason I've stayed.

I know I am doing the best I can within the limitations presented to me but often ask myself if I can do more. Almost everyone working in the aid business suffers from guilt and misgivings during the most trying of times, and I am no exception.

Chapter 9

Family Planning

Early in the response to the refugee crisis, numerous volunteers from all over the world poured into the camps. With little co-ordination or oversight, this influx resulted in a duplication of services, but no specific family planning services for women. Women of all ages came to my little hut office and shyly ask me for "that pill" or "that shot" that prevents pregnancy. In my focus on vaccinating children the lack of family planning services for women had not occurred to me. Refugee women at Khao-I-Dang Camp arrive in various stages of pregnancy; hence the 800 new births reported in the first months of the camp's opening.

My queries at the Medicins San Frontieres Maternity Ward confirmed the unavailability of family planning services but I did learn that abortion services were available. A prominent sign in Khmer, French and English directed me to an air-conditioned enclosure containing an immaculate six cot ward. Every cot was occupied. The staff of one doctor and two nurses welcomed me and explained their equipment and procedures. Sponsored by a Norwegian charity and granted permission by the International Red Cross Committee, they have only been in KID for two weeks. The doctor declined to tell me the number of abortions performed during this time, but claims "Many women come and we are always busy. Let me show you our equipment." I am aghast to learn that abortion services have been given priority over pregnancy preventive services.

Although fully aware that refugee women are at high risk of sexual assaults resulting in unwanted pregnancies, UNHCR does not include condoms or oral contraceptives in their emergency aid supplies. Young girls, aged 12 to 16, are particularly targeted by the Thai soldiers who surround the camp. They are free to enter the camp at night when fewer aid workers are present. When impregnated, usually against their will, these girls bring shame upon their family members. One young girl, looking younger than her claimed 13 years, appeared at my "hut-office" one morning. She asked for my help as she had been "thrown away" by her father. With the help of Yat Nei, my assistant, we found refuge for her in the Unaccompanied Children's Center.

At the next weekly UNHCR/VOLAG meeting, I find others who agree that Family Planning Services should be a priority project. Although the Khmer had lost many children during the difficult years they had endured, the time was not yet right for them to reproduce. Many young women are still ill and undernourished, poor conditions for pregnancy. Attention needs to be focused on the children they already have. An overcrowded, unsanitary refugee camp, combined with an uncertain future, was not the place to bring more babies.

Strong opposition to offering contraceptives to the Khmer women came from the Baptist and Catholic representatives. They argued that the women wanted and needed to have many babies to replace those that were lost. These unrealistic comments disturbed me. I asked, "Would you choose to be pregnant in this camp: would you encourage your wife or sister or daughter to bring a new baby into this hazardous, unhealthy environment?" The six men and women left without answering the question.

The Thai authorities publicly comment on the burden the many victims of genocide had brought on Thailand. They frequently criticize the lack of Family Planning Services and declare "Refugees should return to their own countries to rebuild their population-not here in our country!"

The lack of family planning services quickly became an issue for the voluntary agencies, with differing opinions hotly debated. The Thai Red Cross, providing medical services in Sa Kaeo and many of the smaller camps, report they are providing the Depo-Provera injectable contraceptive to any female, of any age, upon request. Another Thai organization, Community-Based Emergency Refugee Services (CBERS), are providers of vector control, water and sanitation services in the camps. They now offer to initiate family planning services as well.

Strategies used by CBERS are questioned by some of the western-oriented relief organizations. CBERS personnel were familiar with the problems of working with people living under harsh conditions. Although their methods appeared to be unorthodox to outsiders, they proved effective. Their program is initiated in a unique manner. CBERS staff throw brightly colored condoms to refugee males and children, inviting them to "blow up the balloons". They then announce the showing of movies.

An oversized movie screen is set up and popular Asian movies are shown. The films attract thousands of viewers eager for some form of entertainment. Between films, announcements are made that family planning services would be available the following day. The response is overwhelming. Within three days in the Sa Kaeo Camp, 2,252 women of the 10,000 married women sought family planning services. In Khao-I-Dang, the contraceptive prevalence rate jumped from zero to two thirds of eligible women within a week. 95% choose the injectable contraceptive, Depo-Provera.

Much to my embarrassment, those "balloons" kept showing up around my "hut-office". My gang of errand boys competed with each other to see how big they could blow them up. The "balloons" quickly burst with the resulting debris left near my office entrance. This provided extreme hilarity for my colleagues, who, like the refugees, were always eager for some form of entertainment, especially at someone else's expense.

Chapter 10

Reasons To Stay?

Am I tired? Am I homesick? You bet I am. My (old?) practical self tells me it is time to go home and get on with my 'real' job with the health department and being a "real" mother to my young adult children. But---once rested and back in a routine, will I become restless? Remembering how much more challenging and fulfilling and exciting it was living and working in Thailand, will I want to stay home?

Living and working with the many dedicated doctors, nurses and volunteers from 20 different countries; communicating in ways that by-pass language and cultural differences, is both educational and exhilarating. Dr. John Naponick, another American, has been working away from the U.S. for four years. We have many conversations exploring the pros and cons of this lifestyle, and I become increasingly convinced that this is where I really want to be at this time of my life.

My friendship with Suk Mai is beneficial in many ways as she always seems to know when influential and important VIP's are in the area. Suk Mai arranges meetings with Thai Red Cross officials as well as several area military officers that contribute to my "ease of access". I am also making connections with key leaders in UNICEF, UNHCR and International Committee of the Red Cross. My acquaintance with Sheppie Abrambowitz continues as, she, with her group of volunteers, visit the camps weekly. On one visit she accompanied First Lady Rosalyn Carter and group on a fact-finding tour and, as promised, Sheppie arranged that I meet this sincere and true humanitarian. Mrs. Carter is well-informed as to the refugee situation and asked many questions about my immunization program and its needs.

The International Rescue Committee offers me a six month contract, extending both my assignment and responsibilities. In addition to the KID program, I will also be responsible for oversight of disease surveillance and control in six camps in southeastern Thailand, and the 10 year old Laotian Camp in Nong Khai, in Northern Thailand. The refugees in these camps include Viet Namese boat people, displaced Chinese from Cambodia, and Black Thai from the Cardamon Mountains. I accept this contract and a concurrent one with World Concern to write a standardized manual for public health nurses working in the camps.

Once again, I am on that now-familiar road to Bangkok, bumping over klongs, swerving around motos and water buffalo, and spotting the occasional elephant plodding on the side of the road. I happily anticipate a well-earned R & R Week, but this time with assurances that I will be returning to Aran and my work with the refugees.

I stay in a lovely, modern, securely fenced, seven bedroom home that International Rescue Committee has leased for their staff's use. The house is beautifully furnished, with private air-conditioned bedrooms, flush toilets and complete household staff. I feel like a 'princess' and so fortunate to be in this place, doing what I enjoy so much, with others who share the same commitment. There is also a van with a driver for our use, which is more convenient and safer than taxis and buses but I am determined to be independent and learn my way around –by myself. And do so--somewhat----

My first stop is to a dressmaker's for measurements, and to select materials for new clothes—my own designs for cotton blouses and the wrap-around skirts that will keep me both cool yet properly covered. Within two days I have four skirts and eight blouses and then I splurge and have two Thai silk dresses made for my more "formal" occasions. My shopping list is long as Yat Nei, my Cambodian "medical secretary", has many requests, as do several of my housemates. I shop and shop—and eat and eat--enjoying myself immensely!

I'm invited for lunch at the U.S. Embassy, and arrive wearing one of my new silk dresses, the emerald green one. Expecting a small group of ladies, I am startled to find fifty women seated around the tables. Our most important guest is Liv Ullman, the current UNICEF Goodwill Ambassador for S.E. Asia. She is part of an activist group on a world tour whose aim is to bring more attention and funding to the Cambodian Refugee Relief Crisis.

Ms. Ullman speaks sincerely of her concerns for the refugee children's protection, survival, education and development; seeming more like a worried mother than a famous movie star. She shares her plans to visit the camps during the following week and I look forward to continuing our conversation.

Finishing both my paperwork to insure my continuance in Thailand and my shopping, I am both physically and emotionally refreshed and ready to return to Aran. My housemates argue that I need more recreation and convince me to join them for a 'night on the town'. We set out to explore several popular nightspots recommended by other volunteers. After a fantastic, typical Thai seafood dinner, with a spicy curry that left us quite thirsty, we go in search of the famous Cowboy Soi (street). This was so-named, we had been informed, because the first bar there had been opened by a retired, American airman, who always wore a cowboy hat.

Despite a few wrong turns, we wander into Cowboy Soi, to find 20 or more brightly lit bars, crammed into less than a quarter block area. Extremely loud music is coming from every bar. There are very, very youthful males and females moving about the soi; both Thai and foreigners. Entering the first bar we come to, I anticipate an American western/cowboy atmosphere. This "bar" is very dark, smoky and noisy but we manage to claim a table for 8. We sit, we peer around, and are immediately surrounded by a dozen young "waiters" and "waitresses". "Wanna dance with me! Wanna play with me! You wanna be my girlfriend? boyfriend?" "Maybe both, at same time!" Ha! "You American? I love Americans!" "Come with me, I am best!" accompanied by giggles and bursts of laughter. It is difficult to tell the males from the females as all wear layers of heavy make-up and similar, much abbreviated costumes. Males and females are dancing with other males, females, and she-males (katoeys) and we're unable to determine 'staff' from the customers. This is definitely not what I know as a 'cowboy bar' back home in Montana!

We spend an entertaining and educational evening bar-hopping in Cowboy Soi: "The Dollhouse", "The Rio", "The Rawhide", "Cowboy 2". I like these bars better because more men and women dance together; at least the women appeared to be female. Two of our male housemates decide to remain when the rest of us returned to the IRC House. They are both scheduled on homeward flights the next day, and I assume they did actually return to the U.S.A.

The next day I am relieved to return to Aran and start my new assignment. I've already begun drafting my Public Health Nurse's Manual, a work in progress wherever I am. The forms for Disease Surveillance, Morbidity and Mortality Reporting have also been completed and I am excited to start my new challenging assignments. The Vaccination Programs will continue under John Horton with the able assistance of our well-trained and enthusiastic Khmer teams. Life is good!

Chapter 11

Live In The Here And Now

I've been in Thailand almost 5 months. I've acclimated to the heat, constant humidity, the spicy foods and different lifestyles. I continue to miss my family but derive great satisfaction from my new freedom and independence. My best Thai friend, Suk Mai, continues to educate me on the nuances of Thai manners and culture, which minimizes my gaffs as I work more with the Thai Red Cross and military. More and more, I am included in get-togethers with the Thais, as well as attending celebrations at the local Buddhist wat (temple). These are usually fund-raisers with music, puppet shows, food, dancing, and fireworks. The Buddhist monks, always in twos, are very friendly and inquisitive; eager to learn about American ways but careful to never touch or be alone with any female, even one old enough to be their mother!

With the initial refugee crisis subsiding, I develop a schedule that balances my work in KID but also allows me a personal life. This lifestyle is not for everyone but is suiting me well at this juncture of my life. My usual day starts at 5:00 A.M. when I hear the roosters crowing just below my window. I carefully open the mosquito netting that surrounds my cot so as not to disturb any "mozzies" that may have settled on the net during the night. Peering at the floor, I determine that my flip-flops are cockroach and gecko free and safe to slip into. These "critters" grow very large here, and are noisy, so are easy to spot. The trip to the 'sanitary' always involves a wait as there is only one to serve 20 housemates. Shaking out my clothes, I dress and join the others for coffee, biscuits and fruit. We line up to board our agency van for the 1 to 2 hour road trip to K-I-D.

This trip can be done in less time. Check-points are changed frequently, as are the military staffs. There seems to be no routine protocol for this "checking" of vans, the occupants or their cargo. Most times we can quickly move through but other times we must wait on the side of the road while the guards sort through our backpacks and cargo. I am grateful to Vu, our driver, for taking charge with a calm demeanor, and answering questions for us. At times I think I have seen "paper" (money?) passed from hand to hand, and decide that, perhaps, it is safer not to question what I don't understand.

We drive past several Thai villages, check-in at the UNHCR post, and arrive at KID, with its estimated population of 140,000 refugees. My "office" is a bamboo hut, with a mat covering a packed-dirt square of ground, where we sit. There are no desks or chairs and my "records" come and go with me, as well as pens, pencils, notebooks and calculators. Hung on bamboo poles is a 5 foot X 5 foot chalkboard, a gift from Johann, a doctor with the German Red Cross.

My Khmer 'staff' of six, sometimes less but often more, await my arrival. There is little to occupy their time so they wait patiently for my arrival, eager to learn any skill that will not only assist me but will also add to their own education. They all desire to learn English. This 'work' also qualifies them for extra rations-a tin of sardines. Yat Nei, a 24 year old former medical student, is my 'office manager' and statistician. She is multi-lingual—speaking and writing several Khmer dialects, French, and basic English; the main languages spoken by refugees and many aid workers.

Yat Nei has already collected and tabulated the 24 Hour Reports of Mortality, Morbidity and New Births from the 50 clinics and hospitals, and the 12 Camp Section Leaders. I review them quickly and note if there are significant increases in infectious diseases. Next we check the morgue-a huge, air-conditioned Army tent, with multiple locks. Only the Night Guard and I have keys to these locks but the bodies in the morgue rarely seem to match the number of reported deaths. Today, a young, deceased male is missing and I have no clue as to how or why he was removed, or to where. I revise my numbers, return to my "office" to share hot tea and UNICEF-supplied protein biscuits with the "staff" and plan our day.

Today we have use of a "moto". My 'assistants' take turns as my guide, driver and translator and, with me perched on the back, we visit the hospitals and clinics. Next we zoom into the camp sections to talk with Camp Section Leaders. These trips are both informational and enjoyable as my presence is now familiar and I often am invited to share hot tea with groups of refugees in their shelters. Some are anxious to share their personal stories of the years of horror and loss under the Khmer Rouge, while others are not.

These forays also provide an opportunity for my assistants to search for relatives and previous neighbors, or locate anyone who might have information about them. This search is an on-going activity and one I am glad to share, especially when there is a re-connection.

The day is long, hot and dusty and five hours after arising I am ready for a break in the Staff Room in the ARC Hospital Ward. Safe bottled water, protein biscuits, and fruit are always available here, as well as a cot for naps. Today I attend a weekly meeting at the UNHCR Headquarters, which is surrounded by wire fencing and soldiers. I walk for 30 minutes from my office, spend another

30 minutes in ID PASS checks, and then enjoy chicken-on-a-stick and rice, washed down with iced, milky Nescafe at the Hanoi Hilton Café. As always, there is a visible coating of yellow road dust on everything-tables, chairs, food, and customers, topped by a heavier coating of super-sized black flies.

The Hanoi Hilton Cafe was started by a local Thai family and I do not know why it is so-named. It is popular with all the volags as it is the only café. The soldiers line up and watch us eat, laughing and talking and waving their rifles. The Rumor Mill has that the guns are not loaded. I'm unconvinced this is true as I hear shooting from time to time.

At today's meeting, I once again am requesting information on the authorization and progress of a proposed crematorium. The majority of refugees are Buddhist and prefer cremation, and they have asked me to intervene in their behalf. When KID first opened, the daily mortality rate averaged 20. Those bodies were buried in a shallow rice paddy near the camp perimeter. Now, four or five are added daily. A recent heavy rain has uncovered a large number of the bodies, and with the monsoon rains due to begin very soon, I am concerned with the possibility of disease outbreaks.

Funding for the bricks and mortar for the crematorium has been donated, the labor will be supplied by refugee volunteers and UNHCR has approved the site and structure. The local Thai government is holding up our request with the statement: "We don't want these people to become too comfortable here." When I point out the increasing risk of outbreaks of cholera and typhoid and diarrheal diseases for the near-by local Thai villagers, permission to build is quickly granted.

It is nearing sunset, and time for me to leave. Back at my office, I re-load records and supplies while the staff silently watch with sad eyes. I re-assure them that I will return the next day.

During our conversations, they speak with compulsive urgency about the horrors they have witnessed, experienced, and survived. The terrible events of the past five years have left them with justified feelings of impermanence. What is their future? They do not know, nor do I. Our daily parting is always emotional, with tears and hugs, and all of them walk me to the security gate, holding my hands, touching me, and watching until the transport is out-of-sight. Will we see each other tomorrow? There are no guaranteed tomorrows for my friends.

The IRC transport taking us home had brought the medical staff from Aran to the camp. This team will spend the next 12 hours working in the camp hospitals and will not be allowed to leave until the van returns in the early morning. Our return trip to Aran goes faster as check-points are closed at sunset. Physically and emotionally exhausted, hunched against a window on a narrow seat and oblivious to the noisy chatter of my colleagues, I sleep soundly.

Chapter 12

Artie's Story- Do Adidas Make An American Boy?

I met Artie during one of my visits to the Tuberculosis Treatment Ward when he followed me on my rounds. With his shining eyes and bright smile, he listens intently to my conversations with the American doctors on the ward, and then watches from the doorway as I leave. He claims to be 12 years old but is small, even for an Asian child. Artie sleeps in the same cot as his father, as there are no other family members, and he has no other place to be.

This is an all too familiar story here. After several weeks, the father dies, and Artie is sent to live in a ward designated for Unaccompanied Minors. In this ward, children –from newborns to 18 years of age are clothed, fed and protected while ICRC attempts to locate relatives and reunite families. These children are not considered orphans so are not eligible for adoption.

I had almost forgotten about Artie, as his situation is not unusual, until one morning when he shows up at my office. At first, he would not join the others in the hut, but soon sidled in to sit in a corner, watching and listening with a wide smile. One boy, among so many, but one who stands out from the others. He comes every day, preferring to stay inside rather than join the other children that swarm nearby. Rarely speaking, always smiling, he spends his time copying my writing on the blackboard, or watching Yat Nei working on her reports. Once, he follows me to an Immunization Clinic and asks for 'shots'; and, still smiling, and with my permission, receives three and then the oral polio vaccine. As we are walking back to the office, we pass a hut where haircuts are being given. Art sits on the stool, requests, and receives an "American" haircut---a GI buzz cut!

In short time, Artie learns many English words, and is able to converse with Yat Nei and I at a primary level. We are both amazed at the speed he is learning to read in English. Supplied with a notebook and pencil, he writes words and phrases in Cambodian and then in English. He becomes Yat Nei's 'assistant' and writes long columns of numbers on the blackboard for her. Fascinated with the first calculator he has ever seen, I bring him one for his own use, but have to take it with me each time I leave so it won't be stolen. He understands but says, "I am afraid you can't come back. I am afraid the soldiers will keep you."

Artie does not remember ever being in a school, but must have received some early education somewhere. He talks about his parents, two sisters, and an uncle, but cannot recall where his home was, or how his father supported the family. I feel much sympathy for this bright, young boy and my maternal instincts are triggered. He soon is spending his days with me or other Americans, becoming fluent in American slang and referring to me as "my American mother".

As are all the children, Artie is barefoot, but one day he asks me to bring him new shoes that are not Pol Pot sandals. Pol Pot forbade his people to wear any shoes except those sandals, made from recycled tires. Artie is quite specific in his request for "Aidas shoes-like American boys wear". How did he learn so much about American boys?

Unwittingly, I have assumed responsibility for Artie, and so inquired about the process of sponsorship. Since he is not a "Confirmed Orphan", I cannot adopt him, but I can take him into the U.S. as his guardian. I do not discuss this with Artie as this process is lengthy and I am uncertain as to my departure date.

One morning Artie does not appear when I arrive, and cannot be found at any of the usual places. Yat Nei is sent to search for him and finds him in the German Surgical Ward; sitting on a cot with a young girl who has a fresh plaster cast on her leg. She is introduced as Artie's 16 year old sister who was transferred from the border First Aid Station in Nong Samet where she has left her mother and baby sister.

Artie sits silently on the cot, with his head down. He does not speak, and when I put my arm around him, he moves away. He is not smiling but neither is he crying. I do not know what to say but realize this child is no longer an assumed orphan needing a mother. What I can do is help find his family and bring them to KID, where they can be safely together.

During the week, Artie comes to my office as usual, still smiling but remains very quiet. His mother and 2 year old sister are located in Nong Samet Border Camp, and brought to KID. The mother refuses to stay. When informed of her husband's death, she looks away, and carrying her baby, walks back to the ambulance with her older daughter on crutches. Artie remains by my side, holding his Aidas tied together, kicking at his bundle of clothing and shouting, "I want to stay here-with my American mother!"

I am unable to imagine how they can survive in the rough jungle on the border. Yat Nei informs me that Artie's mother plans to return to her home village near Battambang, Cambodia. According to Khmer custom, Artie, an only son, must take responsibility as the "head of the family". By now, a crowd of refugees and volag workers has gathered, and I sense it is my decision to make. Artie tries to hand me his shoes but I place them back on his shoulder, his clothing bundle on the other, and stuff Thai money in his pocket. With hands clasped beneath his chin, he honors me with a deep wai, and, without looking back, strides to the ambulance and boards.

Having obtained a "Signed Permit" authorizing my entry to Nong Semet, I ride in the next ambulance. Nong Semet, Camp 004, one of several huge encampments on the Thai-Cambodian border, is a turmoil of thousands of sick and starving refugees, waiting to be admitted to one of the refugee camps. It is also a large emergency aid center as many volags have set up feeding stations and treatment centers. I really didn't think I would be able to find Artie and his family but I wanted to see where the Thai-Cambodian border started. Nong Samet is less than an hour's ride from KID and as we near the camp, we can hear automatic gun fire and see Thai soldiers chasing a group of Khmer men away from the camp. When mortar shells fall nearby we drive near a bunker and jump in. We can hear more firing from opposite directions. Several German aid workers, carrying small children with IV tubing in their arms, join us.

Who is shooting what, with which, and at whom? And why? Do the Khmer Serei or the Khmer Rouge have that caliber of mortar? Thai artillery? Vietnamese mortars? I am too numb to recognize the danger we are in, but am very concerned about Artie and his family. I will never know if they had already left this area—or are caught in the crossfire. Over 2 hours pass before we can jump back into the ambulance and drive rapidly back to KID with a full load of more sick and injured refugees.

When we arrive, there are at least 10,000 Khmer silently gathered around the entrance to the camp. Having heard the gunfire, they are looking to see if their relatives or friends are among the wounded. The IRC van is just leaving for the return trip to Aran but wait for me to board. This day has been sad and exhaustive and I look forward to going home—my Thai home, and sleep.

SETTING UP SHELTERS, SA KAEO CAMP, 1979

WATER SUPPLY FOR 100,000 REFUGEES

KHAO-1-DANG REFUGEE CAMP ENTRY W/UNITED NATIONS AND THAI FLAGS

AUTHOR AT K-I-D HEADQUARTERS

SA KEAO CAMP TUBERCULOSIS HOSPITAL

KHAO-I-DANG ORPHANS SHELTER

AUTHOR WITH UNACCOMPANIED MINORS

LIEM SIN CAMP FOR " BOAT PEOPLE"

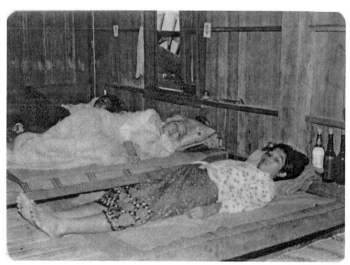

NONG KHAI LAOTIAN HOSPITAL WARD

ART, WITH MOTHER, SISTERS

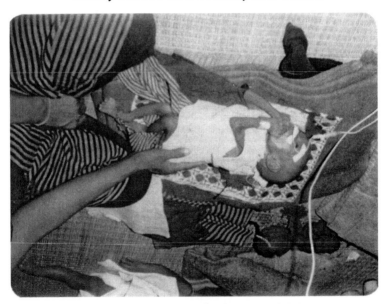

6 MONTH OLD BABY WITH MALNUTRITION, DEHYDRATION

INFECTIOUS DISEASES WARD AIDES

AUTHOR'S "GANG" OF HELPERS

**SA-WA-DEE, MY FRIENDS
I SHALL NEVER FORGET YOU.**

Chapter 13

The Children-The Orphans, The Unaccompanied Minors, And The Veterans

I have come to Thailand primarily because of children; because I have always cared for the very young and helpless who are unable to care for themselves. The longer I work here, the more I learn of the horrific environment these children have survived. Warfare, starvation, disease, and the long, arduous wanderings through the jungles had taken an awesome toll.

Only the more physically robust survived. According to the refugees' own accounts, children who were too heavy to carry and too young to manage on their own were unlikely to survive. Also vulnerable were the elderly and those with debilitating illnesses. The age distribution of the camp population testified to the accuracy of these accounts. Less than 20% of the refugees were under twelve years of age, and very few more than 35. In KID, with a population of 150,000-200,000 that ratio translates into an estimated 30,000 children.

I think of the children I know. Yat Nei has translated many of their stories for me, how they were separated from their families, or forced into a mountain jungle with a brother, sister, or relative, foraging desperately for something edible-a leaf, a sprout, a scorpion, a worm. I imagine their anguish as their siblings and elders weakened, day by day-their panic and helplessness, their sorrow and guilt-each death leaving them more alone. Scraping graves out of the mud with sticks and stones, they wonder what they have done to merit such punishment.

Whenever I have a few spare minutes, I visit one of the children's wards. I feel most needed in the Supplementary Feeding Centre. This is where I brought the newborn twins that had been handed me at the Nong Semet Border Camp when I tried to find Artie. Like all the babies at this Centre, they have feeding tubes in place. They are still so tiny I can hold both of them and another one in my lap at the same time. I caress them and sing the lullabies I had sung for my own children. It is so unfair that these young innocents should suffer. The twins, an estimated three months old, have survived and been given names. But--- what of their future?

I know of at least four families who surrendered their female babies to the Centre because they felt they would have a better life when adopted. This is a real "sacrifice of love", to give up your child in the hope she would have a chance at a better life. Male children are rarely left as they are more highly valued in both the Thai and Khmer culture.

Other small centres for healthy children, under the age of five years, have been developed. No known family members have been located so these children are eligible for adoption. Adoption agencies from around the world arrive to select one or more, but the Queen Sirikit National Institute for Child Health includes an orphanage and has priority. Female children are most desired by Thai adoptive parents and the Queen has declared these children should remain in Thailand, in a culture similar to Cambodia's.

One day I arrived at one such centre to find three Catholic nuns, in their long, grey habits, lying in the muddy pathway in front of a small, white bus. This bus has Thai Royal license plates, a Thai Royal flag on each front fender, and markings indicating that it carried the Queen's representatives. Six well-dressed women, each holding a young baby, are waiting to board the bus. I join the small, silent crowd of expatriate by-standers and refugees and am told that the nuns are objecting to the Queen's representatives removing the children.

A lie-down? Against the Queen of Thailand? Brave-but very risky. Within minutes the nuns are surrounded by Thai militia aiming machine guns at them. They remain lying despite the commands to move away from the bus. Additional militia arrive and the nuns are bodily removed, placed in the back of an Army truck, and the truck drives away.

Eventually, I learn that the nuns, from Belgium, have been working in Thailand for several years. They had to be aware that no one questions Royal Acts. The courageous but misguided nuns were taken directly to Bangkok Airport and will not be allowed to re-enter Thailand.

A unique concept in the care of older, unaccompanied minors in refugee encampments, was developed in KID. Instead of placing these children in a central orphanage, individual "families" of children are created. Mothers who have lost their own children are sought as surrogate mothers for each of these "new" families. UNICEF operated schools, trades training, i.e. sewing, barbering, cooking and clinic aides, for these groups. When they turn 18 years of age, these young adults are free to leave the orphanage, or family group and live in the camp on their own. They could also return to Cambodia, but most remained with their new family group.

With many of the camp residents being adolescents and young adults, a great number had been exposed to little but Khmer Rouge guerrilla life and values since childhood. Not surprisingly, that are often suspicious and hostile when they first enter the camps and confront both the Thais and the Westerners they had been taught to fear and despise. In one incident, when I point out that the medical supplies we are using are stamped "GIFT FROM U.S.A.", I am angrily informed that this was a lie. "Anka (Pol Pot) brought the supplies and you have stolen them." As the weeks pass, more trust slowly begins to emerge.

One ward, dubbed the Veteran's Ward, is separated by fencing from any other Children's Ward, or any known Khmer Rouge living in KID. These boys, aged 8 years to 16 years, are considered "dangerous" as under Pol Pot they had been taken by the Khmer Rouge to serve in the army. They are fearful and combative, refusing food and medical care. Attempts to talk with any one boy is met with fixed stares and silence. On one occasion, when I persisted in making conversation, the 10-12 year old boy-soldier shouted," You are American, Pol Pot hates Americans. I hate Americans! Americans bomb Cambodians!" (Translated by Yat Nei who accompanied me, always.)

Some are reticent to talk of their past experiences while others seem eager to do so. One quite likeable translator shared his experiences as an executioner for the Khmer Rouge. He claimed to have beheaded countless enemies. When asked to define who this enemy was, he replied "You, and you. Our leaders told us everyone not with him was the enemy and to trust no one else."

Even though these refugees were members of the Khmer Rouge, virtually all could tell of the murder and scatterings of their own families. Children, as young as 5 years old, have been found in deserted border villages, the only living persons among the grotesquely strewn corpses. The children are encouraged to draw pictures of their life before they arrived at the camp. Almost always, soldiers pointing guns, and fallen, bleeding figures are depicted.

One can only speculate on the future of these seriously handicapped and homeless individuals; their tragically disrupted lives in a tragically disrupted society. Their future is further complicated by being identified with one of the most brutal regimes in history. What will become of these boys? The plight of these children depresses me. Will there ever be an end to wars? Perhaps if the leaders of countries who make those decisions are required to volunteer in refugee camps, see these children, listen to their stories, maybe, just maybe, they would change their minds--

Chapter 14

Party-Party-Party!

I've been here almost 6 months. Many of the short-term "thrill-seekers" have departed now that the initial crisis situation has receded. There are more longer term 'staffers', like myself, older, more experienced and dedicated to seeking practical solutions for the refugees confined in the 14 camps. The unresolved border situation continues in turmoil, but the camps have reached maximum capacities and are unable to admit more.

Time flies by as I keep busy with surveys and meetings and reports. I'm actually keeping a diary now as there is little predictability and each day brings new challenges. I can't remember when I've ever worked so hard and felt so fulfilled. I have a 'social circle' of friends, and a "social life", different and more exciting from my previous 'home' one.

This "social circle" represents many nationalities-French, German, Scandinavian, Italian, British, Thai, and the occasional Aussie. Discussions become heated and someone will march off in a temper; usually a French volunteer. It seems a party starts whenever two or more people are seen together, which is about always in a household of twenty. Other volag's houses are near ours and people wander between them; carrying food, beverages, music cassettes and tape players. The beer of choice is Sing-Ha, 6 % alcohol and available only in 1/2 liter bottles. The alternate beverage is Mekong whiskey, advertised to be "no more than 1 month old!" I've found that it burns with a bright, blue flame and is also useful as a flying insect deterrent!

The nearby Buddhist Temple has week-end festivals with performances by local bands so a group of us often wander over and join in. We are always welcomed with great fanfare. I suspect we are part of the entertainment as the locals stand apart and watch us dance, then imitate our steps with much behind-the-hand giggling. Michael Jackson and John Lennon's music ("Imagine") is well known here, as well as Madonna's ("Like A Virgin") and Cher's "Jingle Bell Rock" was a hit at Christmas ---and is still played, and sung, with the same enthusiasm—and "The Beat Goes On"----and on---and on.

It is a Saturday and I'm invited to an overnight Farewell Party for members of the Israeli Team—my early rescuers in Sa Kaeo. Six members will stay on, six will leave. The team replacements have already arrived. This team continues to work in the Khmer Rouge-dominated camp, the most dangerous of all the camps. Mick and Danni, my old colleagues, collect me and we drive for an hour to the Israeli Team House. This house is the largest I've seen here, but not typical "Thai" as it is not elevated. It is in a compound surrounded by a 12 foot high wire enclosure, with huge lights on every post, and patrolled by gun-carrying security guards. Entry is by invitation only. Although accompanied by Mick and Danni, I am required to submit my identification papers and a body pat-down before I am allowed to enter. I understand the precautions, but it does put a damper on my party mood.

Eventually, 10 more guests arrive and we swap "war stories." Although we are all working with refugees, we are in different areas and have never met before. It is stimulating to exchange information and discuss mutual concerns. I am scheduled to visit several of these camps soon and look forward to the possibility of seeing my new friends and colleagues again to continue our conversations.

Meanwhile, the sun has set and my Israeli hosts start their party. There are musicians playing violins and drums and a flute. We move out to the yard, and eat grilled lamb (chawarma) and shish kabobs, chick pea dip (humus), yogurt cucumber salad (keyehral lubin yogurt), stuffed zucchini (kousa mahahie), tabbouli salad, and freshly baked flat bread. Everyone is taking turns churning ice cream in a very old fashioned churn. It is similar to one my grandmother has had for years; which reminds me of home and I am suddenly and surprisingly homesick.

My bout of nostalgia disappears when the dancing begins. I join in the ladies circle as the men link arms and move around us in their own circle. We separate, come together, and separate again. The music slows and six or so men come to the middle of the circle, dancing around each other. As the music is played faster and faster, the men link arms. They leap higher and higher, twirling and shouting and laughing, challenging each other to jump even higher. I recognize my friend Mick, who is easily the oldest in the group— leaping the highest!

The sun is barely rising in the East as I finally find a vacant sleeping mat, and sink into a deep sleep. I wake up five hours later, sensing I am no longer alone, and roll over to find both Mick and Danni, and a young female on the mat with me. They are sleeping soundly but wake up while I am trying to disentangle myself, and pull me down again. Mick jokingly reminds me that this isn't the first time that we woke up in the same "bed"; referring to their rescue of me in Sa Kaeo Camp when I first arrived.

Everyone is now up, eating and drinking, and making arrangements to return to their own lodgings. In the middle of the music, conversations, and laughter, an ear-splitting siren goes off and suddenly the Israel Medical Team is standing at attention at the Main Gate. Several have guns. The security guards, with raised machine guns, are at each of the four gates.

The other guests and I are instructed to remain inside the house. The doors are locked and the inside shutters closed and bolted. We are provided with food and water, but are unable to inform our own Team Leaders and houses of our "detention". My failure to return as scheduled will cause concern among both my housemates and Camp Staff. We do not see our hosts again until early Monday morning when they unlock the doors and escort us into the sunlight.

Everyone is exhausted. We "detainees" are nervous and concerned as to the cause of our detention. Mick explains that the Israeli Embassy in Bangkok had received terrorist threats late Saturday night, and the officials were concerned that this Medical Staff Compound –although 300 Km away-could also be targeted. We were told that the "lock-down" was a standard procedure since the attacks on the Israeli Olympian athletes in Munich in 1972. We visitors were "detained" for safety reasons, but are now free to leave.

I arrange transport with another guest and with great relief I soon arrive back in my Thai home. Everyone is curious to hear about my "wild week-end" and the reason for my delayed return. It is not what they think. I am reluctant to share the real story as I need time to process the events of the weekend.

Back in Montana, the only guns I see are used for hunting big game and shooting predator animals attacking our livestock. Here, there are military guns everywhere and I have not become comfortable with this reality. Since arriving I have seen numerous gunshot wounds. The children draw crude, explicit pictures of uniformed men with guns shooting at them and other people..

I resolve to adjust my perception of guns as "killing machines" and try to accept them as necessary protectors.

Chapter 15

In The Merry Month Of May

Dr. Rangaraj, UNHCR Health Co-ordinator for Thailand, has invited me on a tour of refugee camps in Southern Thailand and I'm both nervous and excited. Dr. Raj (as he prefers to be called), is a renowned epidemiologist and public health specialist from New Delhi, India. As he is very energetic, he appears much younger than his age (60+) and many years of experience would indicate. I expect to learn a great deal about international public health issues during our tour of five selected camps, which will include Vietnamese "boat people", ethnic "Black Thais" and Laotians. Since the beginning of the Viet Nam War, Thailand has been overwhelmed with "displaced persons" and the government is begging for help. More aid will be facilitated when the United Nations High Commission for Refugees declares these "illegal persons" legitimate refugees, eligible for protection, shelter, food, and medical care.

We will also try to visit a newly-reported small encampment of Khmer-Chinese seeking refuge. Due to their mixed ethnicity, they were badly treated by the Khmer Rouge and claim that many were murdered. This group escaped to the border; and for the past 4 years have been moving constantly and hiding in the jungles in south-eastern Thailand.

Our Survey Team includes two medical consultants from Germany and Switzerland, representing ICRC and IRC. It is expected that Thai Red Cross officials and staff will join us in each district we visit. I anticipate lengthy discussions due to language barriers and, not for the first time, wish I was learning to converse in Thai at a faster rate. I am also wishing for another female on this team as I've found that males in a group tend to treat me less as a professional equal and more as their clerk. I've already fought and won that equal rights battle at home.

CHANTABURI

An exhaustive nine hour drive brings us to Chantaburi, the closest town to Laem Sin Camp where the Vietnamese boat people have been confined. During the long journey I tried to concentrate on sights on the right of the road rather than the terrorizing view of what was happening in front of our transport. The congested roads varied from dirt-rutted tracks and lumpy pavement to level asphalt, but were always congested and noisy. Local villagers in sarongs and Levis jostled for space amid water buffalo, vintage vehicles, tuk-tuks and motorcycles. Nevertheless, our driver drove rapidly; only slowing for waddling ducks and slow-moving dogs. My efforts to sleep were unsuccessful.

Chantaburi is a small town; a typically dreary, dusty place with the customary enormous wat dominating the center. Our small, one level hotel is located with a spectacular view of the Gulf of Siam's blue water, which appears refreshing after our long drive. A short walk leads me to those cool, blue waters and I have an overwhelming urge to jump in. A longer look reveals a drift of plastic bags, rusty cans and odiferous debris lining the shore. I recall a forewarning about the rampant beach pollution from garbage dumping and open sewage drains and resignedly return to the airless hotel.

Very early the next day we meet with the local Thai Red Cross staff, the responsible agency for the welfare of the "Vietnamese Boat People". They report that this population is now over 2,000 with many sick people, but claim they have neither staff nor resources to care for them. Accompanied by local police officers, the team drives to a low, swampy area about 3 miles from the town. It is a dismal place, with meager, ramshackle tin sheet and bamboo huts, leaning against each other on a dilapidated dock. Extremely emanciated men and women are lying on thin mats, or slouched against a hut. It is very quiet, I smell smoke and can see several small hibachis but there is no odor of cooking food. There are pungent odors of damp and decay, and of excrement, piles of which are noticeable on the small beach, and, of course, the many, many flies which swarm around our heads as we approach.

The few children I see appear sick and malnourished, sitting listlessly and silently. I am dismayed and very angry. These people, who had fled home and country to seek a better life, who found the courage to attempt an ocean journey in small boats, were now being treated with less dignity than animals.

No one on our team speaks Vietnamese, but Hendrix, our Swiss doctor, calls out in French, while I try American greetings. Hesitantly, several men appear and greet us in both French and English. There is no clean place to sit and when we try to leave the compound with the men, the police, with pointed guns, send us back. So we stand downwind on the beach and ask our questions.

Some boat people have been here for as long as 6 months, many have died, of fever, starvation, and "injuries". Injuries include gunshot wounds, beatings, rapes, and drowning. There are several Vietnamese doctors but they have no drugs or medical supplies. Their requests to the local Red Cross for supplies and/or medical care are denied. Pregnant women and sick children are also denied care.

A Memoir—Delivering Health Care in Cambodian Refugee Camps, 1979–1980

We are told of the women who were raped by Thai pirates during the ocean crossings. Several are pregnant as a result of the rapes. In Asian culture this situation brings dishonor on the entire family so the women are "disowned". It is assumed they also have sexually transmitted infections as a result of the rapes. After several attempted suicides, and three successful ones, the women were "confined" to one hut and placed under "guard". My first and second requests to visit this 'hut' are ignored but I persist and on my third request, am escorted to the hut. I find 23 females, mostly very young girls, (12? 15?) crammed into a space so small they had to take turns to sit and/or lie down. Four tiny, unscreened openings in the walls allow limited air and light. Several were obviously pregnant and others were as obviously mentally and/or emotionally disturbed. This "safety" hut, the last one at the end of the row, is easily accessible by road and by water, and I suspect is well known to the police, the military, the local males, and, as well to the Thai pirates. I am horrified and sickened by the whole, obscene situation as I surmise that someone---the police, the military, or even one of the refugees---is collecting payments at the expense of these poor women.

On our return to our hotel, Dr. Raj and I stop at the Red Cross Office. Dr. Raj demands that their captain immediately provide medical supplies and care to the sick refugees, reminding them that many may have contagious diseases which can be transmitted to the local people. My attempts to discuss the conditions of the women are ignored, and I sense I have offended Dr. Raj with my persistence. Back at the hotel, the team writes our report, with recommendations for immediate UNHCR intervention. With U.N. designation of "Refugee Status", Dr. Raj can authorize an emergency delivery of food, water and medical supplies within the next 24 hours to the "Boat People", and sends telexes to his staff in Bangkok to initiate these orders.

It is a privilege to be included in these actions; learning firsthand how to evaluate a crisis situation, to prioritize and authorize appropriate actions with experienced colleagues. When I ask what we will happen with the "confined" young women, I am taken aback to receive the abrupt response of "They will receive medical care with the others." I suggest that they be moved elsewhere so they can be protected from further sexual abuse but am informed that any such action is beyond our authority. I am unable to understand this 'selective' non-action at this time. I need more information-------and add Mrs. Abramowitz's name to my list of "Bangkok Calls".

Chapter 16

Trat And Mei Rut

A new day, and early on the road to Trat, a small city further south. The Gulf of Siam appears larger and bluer and the thickly forested Cardamons Mountains on the Thai- Cambodia border loom in the east. The refugee camp of Mai Rut lies near a fishing village at their base.

Our first 'situation' occurs when we try to register at a modern, three story hotel. This hotel is the newest and largest one I've seen outside of Bangkok. There are no elevators. We do not relish carrying numerous boxes up the many, steep stairs so our driver requests rooms on the ground level. The hotel clerks are adamant that we use rooms on an upper floor. Grinning widely, and 'eyeing' me, they repeat loudly, in fractured English, that "ground rooms are 'hourly' rooms" and you no can have unless you pay more –much, much more." I am totally confused by this conversation, and Dr. Raj's words confuse me even more. With obvious discomfort, he apologizes to me, and orders the young men to also apologize to me.

With an exaggerated show of dignity, the young men wai (bow) and profusely mumble their apologies, leaving me still puzzled as to the 'why'. More staff appears to carry our boxes and baggage up the long, steep stairs. I wait to follow but when I arrive at my designated room, I find Dr. Raj's baggage in my room. Apparently, staff is unaccustomed to 'single female travelers' and assume that I am somebody's spouse. Then I realize that their first assumption was that I was 'for hourly hire', and convulsed with laughter, I flop on the bed. This trip is proving to be educational in many, many ways and I realize I have much to learn about the Thai, and their customs.

Our days always start early and today we started even earlier as we must make necessary, formal visits to the Municipal Police, the Thai military commander, and the District Red Cross Chief. Official visits are always lengthy affairs, and although I've familiar with the protocol, I would prefer spending my time in the camps with the refugees.

We begin at the police station. As our arrival is expected, we were aware of being under observance when we entered Trat yesterday. Without permits, we cannot visit the camps. It is the Thai custom to make visitors wait for officials, especially if you are non-Thai. I suspect the longer the wait, the greater is the official's status. We remove our shoes, drink many tiny cups of hot, jasmine tea, receive instructions on 'kraab' (kowtowing) and wait an hour.

Through the door, I can see the Chief of Police sitting on a small, raised dais. Keeping our heads below the Police Chief's, we crawl on our knees to his dais. Our hands are closed beneath our chins (wai) and, once in place, the soles of our feet are tucked out of sight as it is an insult to show them. Dr. Raj is first in line, followed by Hendrick and John. I'm last.

The welcome speech is delivered in rapid Thai, followed by a long English translation. We each respond with our name, title and organization, and wait while this information is translated into Thai. We are instructed to back out on hands and knees, with heads down. I'm last to go and steal a peek at the Chief. He's smiling; so I smile in return. We receive our permits and depart for the Thai Red Cross Compound.

This compound includes a hospital, an out-patient clinic and offices. It is lunchtime and we are invited to join the staff in their dining room. It is considered rude to discuss business affairs while eating so two hours pass before we are free to discuss the local refugee situation. It is reported that the Khmer refugees in the Mai Rut Camp receive "good medical care, food and housing" but no one is willing, or are unable to name the NGO's providing these services. The Black Thai group was placed in a separate area in the same camp "for their protection". Their dialect is thought to be Khmer-Thai but no interpreter has been found who could translate so they have been unable to communicate with them. They claim to have no knowledge of the Khmer-Chinese group that is reportedly in the same area.

As we prepare to make our last official visit to the Military Commander responsible for this district, we are surprised when he joins us at the Red Cross Office. He speaks fairly good English and actually seems happy to see us. We are invited to his headquarters and we follow him to his unusually spacious office. Offered a choice of Johnny Walker Black whiskey or Sing-ha beer, I drink more jasmine tea.

The General has many questions about our purposes for this visit to his area. Dr. Raj speaks for the UNHCR and the team's mission to locate refugees and assure their care. As with the other two offices, we had temporarily surrendered our passports. As we receive them back with entry permits allowing us to travel in all areas, the General looks at mine and shouts "I know you! My cousin is Suk Mai!" It is a small world.

We politely but firmly decline his offer to accompany us to the camp. A military escort would surely interfere with free discussions with the refugees; who are understandingly distrustful of anyone in military uniform.

MEI RUT/BOREI ENCAMPMENT

The monsoon season has begun and we drive through heavy downpours to Mai Rut. The paved road ends and we leave our van to push through ankle deep mud to the camp security gate. This gate is wide open. There are no security guards but we are greeted by mud-splattered children loudly repeating "Hello! How are you?" Further along are a row of open-front wood-sided "compartments" with charcoal hibachis spiraling smoky fumes into the air. Clumps of people are huddled together inside these areas, silently watching as we slog through the mud. I approach a small group of women, making a deep 'wai' (bow) and "sa wa dee" (greeting). My courtesy is returned with blank stares so we move on. Following the children and the assumed road, we find the guards and a dozen others, tugging, pushing, whipping and berating a pair of mud-splattered water buffalo, yoked to a pick-up truck.

All of us, except Dr. Raj, who watchs and shouts advice, join in the rescue of the supply vehicle. We finally make it to the gate and receive our Security Passes from the guard. We are introduced to Dr. Antone from Medicins San Frontieres and Sister Cecile from Catholic Relief Services, the lead agencies for the camp. It continues to rain heavily so we stand together on a small, elevated platform and let the warm rainwater wash off the muck.

Under cover and fortified with hot tea and protein biscuits, Sister Cecile and Antone inform us that they only arrived two weeks ago. They estimate a population of 6,300 Displaced Persons awaiting verification of refugee status from Thai officials. There are insufficient medical supplies, food rations, shelters, latrines, clothing, relief workers and transport. Rain water is collected in buckets and used for drinking, cooking, and washing.

It is assumed that the group of newest arrivals are the Black Thai we had heard about. They have segregated themselves.

Short and chunky in stature, they appear healthier than the other refugees. The women wear distinctive black turbans, pants and skirts and both men and women blacken their teeth. This group speaks a dialect that is unknown to anyone in the camp or area so communications are conducted through mime and gestures.

We decide it is too late for us to return to Trat, so we drive to the nearby fishing village with Antone. He stays with a local family there. After the customary check-in with the local Police Captain, we are invited to stay---at the Police Station. The jail cells are unoccupied so we have a choice of cots. The villagers of Mei Rut do not receive many visitors and are very friendly, inviting us to join them for dinner on the docks. After a change to dry clothes and a short nap, I wander towards the bay. This village is sandwiched between the heavily forested Cardamon Mountains, which are in Cambodia, and the Gulf of Siam, which is in Thailand.

The rains have stopped, the sky is blue again, and there is a fresh breeze. It is tranquil; the sound of water lapping against the docks, many small fishing boats in the harbor, and the delightful odor of frying fresh fish in the air. I follow the sound of voices and music to the dock and join my teammates and Antone at a long table. Four other MSF volunteers are there also, and, amid much laughter, we have a lively, multi-lingual conversation. Our delicious dinner is freshly caught fish, rice, and vegetables and we finish with local fruits. Everyone becomes very quiet as we watch a spectacular, multi-colored sunset, and the fishermen and their small boats sail out of the harbor, one by one, for their night of fishing.

As we walk back to the jail, we are followed by eight or ten youths, in uniforms similar to the guerilla warfare costumes I'd seen in war movies. They are conversing, and singing in Vietnamese. What is this? We arrive at the Police Station. The

Captain greets us and the 'soldiers' and then distributes machine guns to the soldiers, who proceed up the path towards the mountain still singing.

I wake up and am relieved to view blue skies and bright sunshine through the barred window. Again, the aroma of frying fish permeates the air. I see the fishing boats have returned to the harbor and the fishermen are unloading their night's catch. The mountain side is clear today and I look up to see small fires burning beside bunkers. Vietnamese flags are waving in the breeze along with what appears to be laundry. When I am noticed by a group of soldiers, they wave at me and shout loudly, and I wave back, assuming their greetings are friendly. The Police Chief confirmed this assumption as he claims there have been no shots fired in the six months since their arrival. He does not know the purpose of their presence, but encourages their visits to the village, making certain they check in their guns on arrival.

The rains have retreated, for now. We are able to tour Mei Rut Holding Centre, and assure the staff we would promote their request for Refugee Status for this population. It is assumed these Khmer refugees are Pol Pot supporters, therefore distrustful of the volags trying to help them. With no contact with the world outside of Cambodia for the last 5 years under Khmer Rouge rule, their suspicions are understandable.

Som Tow, our multi-lingual (Thai + dialects, Khmer, French, German and English) driver/translator addresses the 'Black Thai' villagers but they retreat and stare blankly at him. We suspect they understand more than they will acknowledge but are as distrustful as the displaced Khmer. When I greet and attempt to engage a small group of women, they turn and start to walk away but stop and listen when Som Tow quietly say "She'll come back another time."

We collect our belongings in Trat and continue driving on to a hotel in Panasnikom in Chonburi Province. Having been educated as to the folly of requesting first level rooms, here we settle on second level rooms. Dr. Raj's luggage again ends up in my room, and once again I place it outside my door. This is becoming tiresome.

The next day, we repeat the expected formalities as we did in Trat. I'm becoming quite adept with the 'kowtowing" but these officials aren't smiling as the others did. We locate the Panasnikom Holding and Processing Centre, a new, modern building with a current population of 6,541. These refugees are Laotian, Khmer and Vietnamese, with a small number of mixed race children. They have relatives and/or friends who are willing to sponsor them so they are being processed and approved for settlement in another country rather quickly.

Chapter 17

Bangkok--Refugee Status Conference

After weeks in the relatively, quieter countryside, it is a shock to all my senses to arrive in traffic-congested, noisy, smoggy Bangkok. It is raining heavily as Somtow navigates around vehicles, pedestrians and samlors (man powered rickshas) through crowded, narrow, flooded sois (streets) to emerge at the Royal Thai-Sheraton on the Chaphraya River. We are here to attend a UNHCR Refugee Status Conference. Descriptions of this luxury hotel, located near several famous tourist destinations, such as the Golden Buddha and the Royal Grand Palace, are not exaggerated. I'm informed King Rama IX and Queen Sirikit do actually live in their Palace not far from here.

I've also been told that this hotel resembles the palace and I, not ever seeing any palace, believe this must be true. As we enter the spacious lobby, we are greeted by hotel staff dressed as if they had just wandered off the set of "The King and I". I look around for Yul Brenner and spot a near-likeness at the elevator. In a daze I follow a bellhop, carrying my well-worn, stained backpack, to the elevator and up to my spacious room on the 6th floor. No other's luggage is in my room. There is a platter of fresh fruits surrounded by a mass of tiny lavender orchids; and a two page Conference Agenda on a small ornate, gilded table. Jolted back to reality, I recall I am here to attend meetings, and report on conditions in the refugee camps we have recently visited.

A long, hot bath followed by visits to the hotel's beauty salon and dress shops make me presentable for the first event. This is a cocktail party given by the Japanese Embassy to honor their medical team (JMT) and volunteers (JVC). It is a most enjoyable but also beneficial as I am able to talk with Sheppie from the U.S. Embassy and several of the women who are volunteering in Khao-I-Dang and Sa Kaeo. After relating my findings in Laem Sing, and detailing the conditions of the ill and mistreated girls and women, I am assured there will be rapid response and action.

The Conference is informative as I learn about the larger picture of refugee relief efforts; especially the co-ordination of multiple international organizations and allocation of funds. Thailand's government is grateful for the assistance as there are an estimated million Displaced Persons and Refugees currently in Thailand with an estimated 50,000 more on the borders. Many Thai villagers are poor and lack clean water, food and health care. They watch their centuries-old enemies receive refuge and "free" goods and services and understandingly question the perceived unfairness.

Thailand's northern borders had been overrun with Laotian refugees in the aftermath of the Vietnam War; and now, the eastern borders with Cambodian refugees. Vietnamese boat people, as I saw in Laem Sing, are arriving along the southern coastlines. There are also recent reports of small numbers of Burmese displaced persons arriving near Mae Sot, on the western border.

Residents of border camps are considered illegal immigrants, and barring unusual circumstances, are ineligible for interview or consideration for refugee status. Residents of camps like Khao-I-Dang and those on the Thai-Laos border, are considered refugees. If they can prove prior connection with the United States during the Vietnamese War, or real danger in returning to their homeland, they are eligible for interview with a U.S. State Department representative. This interview will determine if they are candidates for re-settlement in the United States.

Of particular interest to me are the reports on the impact of starvation—on refugees and relief workers like myself. I have never personally experienced extreme hunger, nor have any of my colleagues, and to witness the degree of starvation among the refugees is shocking. I have not become used to this and feel a stab of guilt when I do eat—so eat less.

An effective exercise is today's "lunch", consisting of the same rations an adult male refugee might receive for an entire DAY: 1 tin of sardines, 1.5 cups of boiled white rice, 2 (1 cup) servings of over-cooked mixed greens, a banana, and 4 protein biscuits—a total of about 900 calories. It is an unappetizing meal and I, like most others around me, did not finish it. I feel deprived but am fully aware that, later, I can eat whatever I want, wherever I want.

Medical textbooks do not tell us how to treat starving patients and surely the psychological management of starvation victims is exceedingly complex. The spectacle of starving persons, especially the children, with their thin little faces, distended abdomens and silence, has had an extraordinary psychological effect on I, and my co-workers. It has caused us to suffer anguish, anger, panic, and guilt. At least two of my former housemates had become emotionally incapacitated and returned to the U.S. before the end of their commitments.

Today is my 47th birthday. I have not told anyone nor have I expected any Birthday Cards from Montana to reach me. Daniel told me of a particular gold shop called "Jonny's Gems", in a soi (street) of "Gems and Gold" shops in the Old Chinese area. It is a popular place with Americans, especially servicemen, and is within walking distance of the hotel.

The shops dazzle me with their array of gold, silver, white and black pearls, sapphires, rubies, and my birthstone, emeralds. When I mention my friend's name at Jonny's, I am welcomed like an old "friend" also, and served jasmine tea and hot noodle soup.

It was difficult to choose but I finally decide on three small emeralds and select settings. When I share the reason for my 'self-gift', Jonny calls his family into the shop. Now I am toasted with a potent, homemade brandy, and returned to the hotel in their private car.

In my room I find a good-sized packet of mail from home, including birthday cards. There is a long letter from JC and his girlfriend, announcing they had moved up their wedding—planned for September, to 01 June--in two weeks! There is no possibility I can be home by then and I am very, very upset with them for the short notice. I really don't feel that this girlfriend is the right person for him but then I barely know her. I will call him in the morning.

The news in my mail has left me hurting and dispirited; and I would prefer to be alone, to think about my life and the direction it has taken. Nevertheless, it is MY birthday and I join Dr. Raj, my teammates and six other "surprise" guests in the lobby. From the hotel dock, we board a boat that will float the Chaophraya River as we dine. There is an overwhelming array and amount of food and we are hungry. Traditionally attired musicians and dancers board at the next hotel dock and I am serenaded with a Thai version of the Happy Birthday song! I am given flowers and small, wrapped gifts, with many "cheek" kisses and hugs. Dr. Raj makes a long speech that both honors and embarrasses me but one I appreciate. How can I remain in my dark mood when my life is being "celebrated" by, and with, such thoughtful friends as these in this lovely place at this particular time in my life?

Where, and with whom, will I be celebrating my NEXT birthday? I recall my own, and all my children's past birthdays with fond memories, but achingly aware that those times are past. My future is my own now and, whatever it is, wherever it leads me, will be my own decision. Not my father's or a husband's, not my children's, and definitely not my former Bureau Chief's----but MINE----all mine!

Chapter 18

Good-Bye Bangkok! Hello Nong Khai!

Calculating a 12 hour time different, I wake early to call my son in Montana. We waste time and money as we both cry. JC defends, his girlfriend's position on the wedding date change, as a matter of convenience for her. He then tries to blame me for not being home to help him make this decision as he feels he is not ready to get married. He's only 24 and hasn't finished college; she has. We set a date and time for another conversation when his girlfriend can join us.

Reviewing the work yet to be accomplished, I anticipate returning to Aranyaprathet and the camps. I'm missing both my colleagues and the camp staff and I am at high risk of becoming accustomed to "luxury living"; hot water tub baths, air conditioning and Western food!

Sheppie joins me for breakfast, along with three women from the American Red Cross, to discuss the situation I had encountered in the Laem Sing Boat Camp. Like me, they are horrified that these young women are being treated in the manner I reported and I am again assured their situation will soon be investigated.

There is a change of plans and I am to accompany Dr. Raj on another camp status assessment. We are to visit a Laotian encampment in Nong Khai, Thailand. This small city is on the Mekong River, directly across from the capital city of Vietiane, Laos. From the first group of 25,000 Hmong reaching Thailand in May, 1975, the number had steadily increased to 60,000 by the end of 1979. It is estimated that close to 3,000 persons are crossing the Mekong each month. There are seven other similar encampments along the Mekong River border but our plan is to visit only this one.

Nong Khai Camp, with a population of 31,724, is the largest of the seven camps designated for the Hmong. During our five hour drive, Dr. Raj patiently answers my many questions about his work with UNHCR. His experience in diverse situations and knowledge of public health is impressive and he encourages me to pursue my own interests in this field.

We arrive too late to visit the local authorities for our passes or to visit the camp, so we find a small guest-house to spend the night. I barely stay awake to finish eating our late dinner.

When I wake up, I am relieved to find that Dr.Raj, who slept on the other cot in the hostel room, has already left. Driving through the crowded streets of this typical border town is challenging as the walkways and narrow road often merge. Som Tow, our driver, weaves through tuk-tuks, small and large animals, hawkers, bicycles and pick-up trucks. Main Street is a bewildering mixture of gold shops and banks with the usual sidewalk eateries and open air, fresh produce markets side by side.

Dr. Raj has obtained our passes to enter the Laotian camp but when we arrive, there are no guards and the rickety security gate is propped open. The monsoon rains have not let up and we splash through puddles of fetid water searching for the Administration Office and the hospital. Glancing around, a two word description of the surrounding miserable thatch and blue tarp huts comes to mind—HELL HOLE. I think I heard these words in a movie and I'm uncertain what the words actually mean but it seems to be an apt description for this place. We find a small wood and tin sheet building with the universal Red Cross symbol and run up the broad stairs. The wide, double doors are locked but tall, narrow windows are open to the veranda. The thunderous sound of rain water cascading down sheet metal roofing muffles our knocking. We put our heads in the window and shout loudly until the door is finally opened by a small boy of 8 or 9 years of age. He stares and quickly runs in the opposite direction before we can ask any questions.

There is no lighting in the long, low-ceilinged room, where 40 narrow cots are arranged in four rows. Every bed is occupied by males, females or children, with at least 10 cots occupied by more than one person; either another patient or family member. In Thailand, it is customary that family members stay with the patient. Four, white-coated women are huddled at the far end; peering anxiously at us.

I approach the women slowly, identifying myself, Dr. Raj, and Som Tow, our driver, and explain the purpose of our visit. We join them in their cramped cubicle to drink jasmine tea and ask questions about the camp and prevalent medical conditions. The patients' records are produced but reveal little more than name, sex, estimated age and 'probable condition'. The doctors maintain the Drug Treatment Records which they take home with them each night. Although they are supposed to cover the hospital 24 hours a day, they come to the hospital together but only in the daytime. They claim they are too frightened to stay here alone at night, leaving the hospital without medical staff after dark and on weekends. They offer no information on camp conditions because, as "clinical doctors", they say they are assigned to provide medical care, and rarely go outside the hospital. Babies are delivered in the family huts by Hmong midwives. They are unaware of any immunization programs.

We are informed that the majority of admissions are for: "respiratory distress, fever, diarrhea, malaria, parasites, malnutrition, and skin diseases". Trauma patients, from fights, knifings, and shootings, and accidents, i.e. burns and too much opium smoking, are taken directly to the Nong Khai Hospital by the Thai Security Police.

This information was relayed with little emotion. My initial experiences in Sa Kaeo and KID were overwhelming as there was no way I could have prepared myself for the plight of those refugees. The relief workers, volunteers and paid staff, arrived to attempt to relieve the refugees' suffering and their physical and emotional status are improving. I am shocked with the indifference of these doctors and Dr. Raj has become quiet; unusual for him. They decline to guide us to the Camp Administrator's office but point the way from the doorway.

Sloshing through muddy puddles, we easily locate the Administration Building, the only one with lighting. Our entrance startles the half dozen or so people gathered around a table and they stop talking and stare at us. Now what? This is Dr. Raj's third visit to this camp and he is recognized by a Thai Baptist Mission volunteer. We sit, drink tea, and share information from the others camps. It is quickly evident that this group feels the recently arrived Cambodian refugees are receiving more attention and better treatment than the Laotians, who have been here for more than 5 years. They have lost staff and funding. Medical and drug supplies have been reduced as well as food rations. They are clearly overwhelmed with their situation.

The rains have lessened so we are able to tour the camp, which doesn't appear any less depressing in better light. This old camp is overcrowded, with garbage piled ankle deep and open fires burning close between the plastic draped huts. Hordes of winged insects swarm up as we walk, and the lethargic refugees stare and do not respond to our greetings. Among the fetid odors surrounding us, the cloying, sweet smell of opium is evident, and we can see opium smokers puffing on their pipes.

Many women are holding babies but older children are gathered at the far end of the camp, where UNICEF is operating a school. There is a shortage of both teachers and supplies; lessons are only two hours daily for each grade level. Children are not required to attend and there are no upper grade classes. Unable to attend school, or to have a job, combined with the breakdown of family tradition and the uncertainly of a future, the young people roam aimlessly about, inside and outside the camp.

Returning to the Administration Building, I have many questions, especially about the absence of Americans. USAID has donated building materials. The permanent volags arrive from Australia, United Kingdom, Norway, French, Italy, Switzerland, and Thailand. Short term aid arrives from various church organizations, i.e. Latter Day Saints, the Baptist Aid Society, and Catholic Relief Services based in Thailand. I am politely reminded of the post-war conflicts of the Viet Nam War that continues to affect Laos and that Americans are neither liked or trusted and may be at personal risk if present in this camp. Nevertheless, Laotians designate America as their first choice Settlement Country!

My first impression is accurate—this place is a hell-hole. The dedicated volags ability to work in this challenging environment is admirable but I can hardly wait to return to Aran. Back at the Guest House, Dr. Raj and I have a lengthy discussion about refugee relief problems in general, and this camp in particular. I am now embarrassed to recall how naïve I was when I asked Dr. Raj for his guidance on continuing in international public health and thank him for his patience with my questions. He has undergone years of specialized training and even more years of 'hands-on' experience in severe disaster response operations. This is my first experience and could well be my only one.

My mentor issues me a challenge: Would you be willing to remain in Nong Khai for a short time to conduct surveys and provide staff training on immunizations and tuberculosis treatment? I am speechless. These are my areas of specialty but I am uncertain if I can adapt routine formats to this awful place, where I sense my presence is barely tolerated.

On the other hand, there are benefits from unique learning opportunities and this is a once in a lifetime situation. I accept Dr. Raj's challenge. Arrangements are quickly made for me to stay in the International Rescue Committee's Staff House in Nong Khai, where the four hospital 'clinicians' live. This house also serves as a Guest House for other 'clinicians' working in Laotian camps in the area. I tell myself that it is only for 10-14 days; surely I can re-adjust my personal negative impressions and provide needed professional services to the Laotians.

Dr. Raj left; I've been here a week and it is too late to change my mind. I'm being stared at again—in the camp, on the street, in the house. The four clinicians, from the Philippines, resent my presence and speak only to each other in Tagalong, a Filipino dialect. Our four Thai house girls stare at me and giggle. At the camp, I am making headway with the volags, who all try to talk to me at once, assuming wrongly that I have greater influence with the international aid agencies.

I've acquired a trio of English-speaking Laotians who claim to be doctors, and assign them to the Tuberculosis Case Files. It appears a hopeless task to determine if any refugee here has actually completed the required treatment regime so it can be assumed that all 11,790 persons here are "active cases" or are "at risk". Any refugee applying for third country re-settlement, has to be free of any active communicable disease. Tuberculosis treatment can take 2 years or more. This fact can be used as an incentive for the refugees to come for chest x-rays and treatments, but the crowded, unsanitary, living conditions also promotes the transmission of tuberculosis, as well as many other diseases.

At the camp, I'm making headway with the dedicated staff. I attend their daily briefings, and insist at least one of the Filipino clinicians attend with me. There are few short-term staffers, as most come for 18-24 months, sponsored by religious and charitable agencies in their home countries. Their commitment is admirable as they work tirelessly under these draconian conditions with little recognition or support from the Thai Government.

Once again, I'm anxious to start vaccinating children. Not surprisingly, there is a high infant and maternal death rate in this camp, mostly from preventable conditions and diseases. I check the vaccine supplies to find about 30% have long passed their "USE BY" dates and pray that the refrigeration has not failed for more than 12 hours at any given time. The four injection guns I take back to the Guest House to clean and test.

The clinicians and I travel to and from the camp by the slow and nerve-wracking, "samlor", which are either leg-powered or motored.

On my 8th day in Nong Khai, I decide to stay 'home' and clean the jet guns, write reports, and explore the surrounding neighborhood. I've seen little of the area in daylight and am surprised to see it a rather upscale one, with large, modern houses, all gated like the one I'm staying in.

The Security Guard follows me around the fenced compound and stares mutely when I ask him about the small, red pick-up parked on the side. It's a Datsun with IRC logos on the doors and a key in the ignition. I climb in, start the engine, shift the gears, and grateful I first learned to drive cars with manual gears, I steer towards the gate. The guard obediently opens the gate for me, I drive through, and he closes it. He then jumps in the back and waits for me to drive away. I have no idea where I am much less where to drive to, so I just maneuver down the narrow, rutted lane. My "freedom run" quickly ends when I meet another car coming into the same lane and I have to back all the way to the gate, with the guard shouting directions—in Thai.

The other vehicle, a van, has IRC logos too, and four passengers. One of them is Dr. Amos Townsend, the IRC Regional Medical Director and the others are with UNICEF. Amos is an American who is in Nong Khai to support and oversee my projects in the camp. They found my effort to escape with the IRC vehicle quite humorous and I have a feeling I will hear about it again --and again. The Filipino clinicians are acquainted with Amos and their English language skills show rapid improvement as we discuss events at the camp.

The next day Amos and I visit the Police Station to obtain my Driver's License. We drink tea, wait, do the 'sompeah' and the 'kowtow', wait, and finally receive a document stamped with elaborate seals. I'll operate on blind trust that this paper allows me to legally drive anywhere in Thailand. After six months of being driven everywhere by someone else, I feel liberated, knowing I can drive myself if necessary.

Time is going by rapidly and soon I can return to Aran. There is better record-keeping for the TB Program and the doctors have recruited "finders". The "finders" bring patients in for chest x-rays and medications. The clinicians are interacting more with other camp volags and assist me in the Immunization Clinics. This camp, and the other six camps designated for Laotians, needs more volunteers in all areas. I'm glad I've had this experience but I would not wish to return.

This experience has also shown me another side of disaster relief responders; those who come for purely humanitarian reasons and those who come for profit. A typical example of profiteering: my housemates from the Philippines who come only for the money they receive. By Western standards their education and training are insufficient to qualify them for medical or nursing licensure but they do practice as such in the Philippines. They are recruited for 3-6 months, with all expenses paid, at a salary of $2,000 per month. Their average salary in Manila may be $3-400.00 per month. With this extra income, they inform me they are able to support a large, extended family and send their children to school. All of these clinicians have been here more than once and plan to return as often as possible.

In contrast, I have worked with highly qualified volags, from the U.S. and European countries, who pay all their own expenses and stay because they are needed. Who am I to judge anyone's motives? I am not comfortable with anyone accepting the benefits but not providing care for those who are in desperate need-----

Chapter 19

Homecoming—Aran

I am so grateful to return to Aran, to familiar places and friends. Suk Mei and her family greet me with deep bows (wai), calling out, "Sa wa dee, Madame Chalot". My proposed 2 week trip had expanded to 6 weeks. I did not assume that there would be no changes during my absence but when Suk Mei showed me my new 'space', in the middle of a row of 10 cots, I was keenly disappointed. Apologetically, she said "So sorry for you. More people come and go, more cots needed, more laundry, more cooking. No time for beauty parlor."

John had sectioned off a corner and installed a custom-made bed to accommodate his 7' height. Noticing my anxiety, he invites me to share his bed, claiming "No problem, there is extra room at the foot." There is also room for a cot to be wedged in the corner so I quickly pushed mine into that space.

That evening, both old and new friends gather on our veranda. At least this space is unchanged and remains the most popular place in the neighborhood. The volunteers now working in the relief operations do not share the initial heart-breaking experiences that defined my first days here but they have come to help wherever they can. I am puzzled when I'm asked how I had celebrated my birthday. "How did you know I had a birthday?" I ask. Everyone is laughing; serenading me with the "Happy Birthday Song" in multiple languages. They point to Daniel climbing the stairs carrying a towering, candle-lit, cake. David follows with a bucket of home-churned coconut ice cream.

Daniel announces, "This is your second birthday cake. We enjoyed eating the first one at your surprise birthday party a month ago. Why didn't you come back to us?" This is my third birthday cake so I cry. "Now I feel like I've really come home!" Everyone is curious to hear about conditions in the other camps I had visited but I'm reluctant to dampen the festive evening with the depressing situations I had encountered. I promise a full report another time.

After the guests leave, Daniel announces he has rented a large, four bedroom house nearby. There is one unoccupied bedroom and he is inviting me to join him and the other four residents. I think, "My own room! Privacy!" To Daniel, I say "Yes, Yes, Daniel! Thank you so much. Tomorrow, for sure as I must go to KID first to see my friends and Khmer staff, and then I'll come." I cannot think of a more welcome homecoming gift-----------------

There are many changes. John is Medical Co-ordinator of 10 camps; and Daniel is Medical Co-ordinator for KID and Sa Kaeo. A Khao-I-Dang- Public Health Department, and a School of Nursing, run by Cambodians, is operational. I agree to teach several courses.

Life is going on as before at the Camp. Departures are common occurences in this unstable environment; among both the volunteers, and other refugees, so when I returned as promised, Yat Nei and our helpers cried and shouted. We drank tea and shared our stories. I made my usual rounds of hospital wards and the huts. KID is looking more like a small city, with schools operated by UNICEF, optical services and glasses provided by KIWANIS INTERNATIONAL, dental services and pocket-sized vegetable gardens.

The Immunization Clinics are now operated by the KID Public Health Department. In my absence, Norwegian Christian Aid has opened a shelter for abused women, and in addition to counseling, also provide contraceptives and abortion services. When I share my experience in Laem Sing's Vietnamese Boat People Encampment, they become interested in providing services there also. I direct then to Sheppie Abramowitz at the U.S. Embassy.

Surprisingly, I'm having mixed feelings. It is rewarding to see the improvements in the overall health of the refugees, and watch them assume control for the programs that are for their own benefit, but---that also means I'm not needed as much as before. I miss the urgency of the first months here but if I'm "not needed" here, I'll have to return to Montana—and I'm not ready to go home-not yet, anyway.

Back in Aran, I spend time with Suk Mai. We re-visit the beauty parlor, purchase a sewing machine for her daughter, now a 'Certified Seamstress', and material for her to sew clothes, first for me. Suk Mai is unhappy to see me leave her house but helps me move my belongings to Daniel's house. When we arrive, we are surprised to see additional cots lined up in the living room.

I find my designated bedroom am surprised to find two people sleeping in my bed. Daniel neglected to warn me that we would have houseguests. He had invited Joan Baez, representing Amnesty International, and Liv Ullman, UNICEF Goodwill Ambassador, to stay in his house, and here they are. In a hammock on the veranda, I find Alexander Ginsburg, the Russian dissident now living in the U.S. He, too, is traveling with the tour group.

Chapter 20

"The Star Trail"

For the next week, life is definitely in the Fast Lane! There are seven people in the entourage, all staying in Daniel's house. I suspect this is the reason he acquired it and I feel fortunate to be in their company. They are part of a group of humanitarians who are traveling to many countries, to raise awareness, and funds, for the Cambodian, Laotian and Viet Namese refugees' relief efforts in Thailand.

It is a pleasure to lead the tour in Khao-I-Dang. Ms. Baez brought her guitar and spends many hours in the hospital and children's wards singing and talking. Ms. Ullman visits the schools and the Red Cross Family Unification Center; encouraging the children to tell her their stories. She becomes very emotional when she hears there are 250 children in our "Unaccompanied Minors Center". These children, from newborn to 18 years of age, have no known family members in KID, but cannot be declared orphans, therefore eligible for adoption, until all efforts to locate relatives have been exhausted.

On the last day of the group's visit, we are stunned to see a shiny, black tour bus driving through the camp. It stops, and a dozen people, each with several cameras, file out of the bus and begin taking photos of refugees, their huts, and our guests. I am speechless, but Mr. Ginsburg isn't. He becomes very agitated, waves his walking stick at them, and demands loudly, in Russian, for them to leave, (I think). They ignore him. I confront them, demanding to know who gave them permission to come here and requesting they leave immediately. I am also ignored.

By now, a small crowd of children, attracted by the shouting, has joined us, pushing in front of Ms. Ullman and Ms. Baez. When several of these 'tourists' began shoving the children away while aiming cameras at the women, the children shoved them back, knocking one to the ground. With the children leading the way, we escaped to a nearby hospital ward.

Later I'm told that an enterprising Thai tourist agency had arranged this "tour", charging high fees for the opportunity to see "real refugees" and 'famous people'. The Thai military guards, responsible for camp security, are questioned by U.N. authorities but deny any knowledge of the tour bus or its operators. They do not have an explanation as to how this over-sized, shiny, coal black bus could pass through the two security gates, manned by these same Thai military guards, without being noticed.

Chapter 21

"Crisis Junky"

I have a feeling that my daily schedule is becoming too predictable, too similar to what I had left behind in Montana. Get up, drive to various camps, attend meetings, teach classes, and write reports. Attend parties and greet newcomers. Saying farewell to co-workers and refugees I have known only a short time but with whom I have shared so many unforgettable moments that our time together surpasses limitations. I suspect I have become a 'crisis junky'; considering a day without drama as one hardly worth remembering!

Dr. Raj reappears in the area with increasing frequency. He informs me, "You think I am too old for you. You need younger men to keep up with you". When he turns his attention to a younger-than-I nurse from Portland, I find it amusing. My own social life is full, and there is, indeed, an array of male companions to choose from, depending on my mood. I've learned to differentiate between playful "geographical bachelors" and those of a "mignon" inclination. Both transvestites and homosexuals are tolerated in Thailand. Since I have no interest in re-marrying, I choose my companions without prejudice, primarily for their conversational skills and dancing abilities. During my younger years I was not allowed to date. During college and nurses' training, I was required to live in a dorm at the hospital with little time or opportunity for dates or parties. At this late stage in my life, I am making up for lost time!

So yes, younger men, like Danny from Tel Aviv, a charismatic pediatrician with sparkling blue eyes, who escaped with me to a rice paddy during a dull party—to dance with wild abandon under the full moon's bright light. I'll always remember Johan, a leprosy specialist from Stuttgart, who sings romantic Bavarian songs to me, and the half-my-age infatuated Frenchman who followed me everywhere until I resorted to ducking behind huts whenever I spotted him first.

Suk Mai has not given up on finding me a 'suitable husband'. She continues in her attempts to teach me the Thai language and customs and introduce me to male relatives and friends, with whom I can barely communicate. Among the many interesting Thai customs, is the one of polygamy—primary and secondary wives. The present King's grandfather, King Maha Mongkut, is claimed to have had more than a 100 wives. Realistically, I suspect my American passport adds to my popularity more than my "good looks" or stimulating conversations.

The 'Public Health Nurses' Manual for Refugee Camps" is almost completed. My two secretaries in the Bangkok office are still learning to type in English so constant editing and re-editing of the drafts is necessary. IRC will finance the printing and distribution as soon as I approve the final edition. My contract is almost finished and I must soon make a decision to remain— or return home. I procrastinate and avoid thinking about that decision as much as possible.

Meanwhile, here I go, again, on a follow-up evaluation trip back to Mei Rut. This UNHCR team is much larger and includes two female consultants, one from Japan and one from Denmark. Dr. Raj again leads the delegation and we travel in a convoy of two vans. These team members, like Dr. Raj, have worked in many crisis situations and they patiently answer my many questions as I continue to learn more about the challenges in international health care. I am inadequately prepared in both education and experience for a career in this field and I'm encouraged to pursue advanced studies in global public health. Several U.S. universities are recommended and they all offer to write Letters of Recommendation for me.

At our first stop, in Chantaburi, we pay our respects to the local Thai Red Cross staff and the Police Chief. They are even less happy to greet us on this visit than our initial visit and the Police Chief politely declined to accompany us to the Laem Sing Boat Camp. This Camp is where we found 23 young women in appalling conditions, sequestered in a locked hut. The Chief confirmed they had been visited by "women from Bangkok" and 20 girls had left with them. Three had refused to leave the Camp.

When we arrive at the Camp this visit, we find conditions have been greatly improved. It is cleaner, the refugees appear less malnourished, and there are basic medical services. The hut that had housed the women is gone, and I receive only blank stares when I ask about it. Was it burned? Washed out to sea? Scavenged for firewood? I'll never know but I can ask Sheppie about the whereabouts of the young women.

Trat appears more modern and less cluttered in sunlight. I recall that it rained continuously during our first visit and there was 'confusion' over room assignments. There was no such 'confusion' this visit at the hotel and I am content with sharing a room with my two female colleagues. Unfortunately, we have a long wait at the Police Station, drinking many cups of jasmine tea. We are informed that the Chief is "too busy for you" and only Dr. Raj and I can receive permits, but no one else. We politely argue but do not receive more than the two permits.

Suk Mai's cousin, the Military Commander, is not in sight. The Thai Red Cross staffs greet us more warmly and we accept their offer to accompany us to Mei Rut Camp. The five vehicles in our convoy create much excitement when we arrive at Liem Sok Village as there are few visitors in this isolated area. More commonly, villagers travel by foot, moto, water buffalo and fishing boat. The local Police Chief remembers us and is unconcerned that we have only two permits for seven visitors.

I look up at the mountain where I had seen the caves and the soldiers during my first visit but the area appears deserted. There are more military personnel around the village, both Thai and Vietnamese, but they are unarmed. When they pass us, they call out loudly "Hello, you Americans? Welcome! Good-by!" They are so young and short in stature, I am unable to think of them as "killing machines" as portrayed in news stories. My sons and their friends look more ferocious in sport competitions.

On the now dry and dusty road, we arrive quickly at the Mei Rut Camp. The inhabitants have obtained refugee status; and receive adequate food supplies and medical care. The wood structures erected to house them are crowded but provide superior accommodations compared to other camps. Every other camp I have visited has only bamboo and/or blue plastic huts. These refugees refuse to apply for third country resettlement, managing to receive food supplies from outside sources. It is confirmed they are Khmer Rouge, refusing to believe that Pol Pot has lost his power; and are waiting to return to Cambodia to reclaim their government and control of the country.

It was undetermined which country the "Black Thai" group belonged and since their status was undetermined, they could not be considered refugees. At the end of the monsoon, the group simply packed up their belongings and walked away. They appeared healthy and self-reliant. They are probably mountain people; living their lives the way their ancestors did, with little interest in the modern lifestyle. There have been no reported sightings of them or of the elusive Chinese-Thai group.

Without a valid reason to remain in this area we unanimously agree to continue driving to Bangkok. Closing my eyes and pretending to sleep during the road trip allows me time to think. It is gratifying to see the progress the refugee relief efforts have made-- so why do I feel so empty? So many people have responded to the calls for help, and we have accomplished much. Now what do I do?

Chapter 22

Flying Tigers And International Organization For Migration

Dr. Raj decides the group should visit the Bangkok Transit Centre, where displaced persons who have been accepted for re-settlement in other countries, await departure. Rangsit Centre is the newest, and although crowded, appears to be quite clean and well organized. Today we are informed that an estimated 110 refugees will be leaving very soon for the U.S. and the anticipation is almost palatable. There is much joy in starting a new life in a foreign place, but also fear in leaving what is familiar: both the good and the terrible times.

I am startled to hear "Madame Chalot, we are here!" and am quickly encircled and embraced by seven shouting and sobbing people." They are a 'family group' from KID, who 'know' me much more than I 'know' them and assume I have come to see them depart. Of course I am happy for them, and try to answer their questions about their anticipated new life in Minnesota. Gazing at their sparse bodies, thin clothing and flip-flops, I keep my thoughts of cold and snow to myself. I have confidence warm coats and boots will be supplied by their sponsors upon their arrival.

The UNHCR Team is staying at the Five Star Dusit Thani Hotel but I prefer to stay in the International Refugee Committee

A Memoir—Delivering Health Care in Cambodian Refugee Camps, 1979–1980

housing. This Guest House is within walking distance of the IRC Offices, which stays open seven days a week; enabling me to finalize the Public Health Nursing Manual. The other advantage is my housemates—newcomers and interesting people to introduce to Bangkok shopping, restaurants and night life in "Soi Cowboy"!

The "Public Health Nurses' Manual" is finalized and sent to the printers. I am loading boxes for the return trip to Aran when Dr. Amos Townsend calls to inform me "Transport is on its way to collect you, forthwith. (A favorite phrase of his). Bring your backpack and travel documents as we are to travel on a Flying Tiger flight to Los Angeles." Six other people with backpacks join me on the driveway where we wait in dazed silence. Dr. Amos arrives and announces we must be at the Airport, forthwith, and "our mission" will be detailed later. Dr. Amos is a retired Air Force colonel and often uses military terms.

Quickly I hustle to claim a seat near Dr. Amos. I'm always open to new adventures but I am clueless as to the purpose of this "mission" and, extremely apprehensive. I'm unfamiliar with a Flying Tiger Airline. Could I possibility be in over my head this time? Agggh--- I do trust Dr. Amos, I think. During the 45 minute ride to Don Muang International Airport, I learn that "our mission" is to accompany 150 Laotian and Cambodian refugees to Los Angeles, CA. Dr. Amos promises to relate the long and interesting history of the Flying Tiger Line during our flight.

International Rescue Committee, our contractor, has "loaned" us to the International Migration Agency (IOM). This organization was born in 1951 out of the chaos and displacement of Western Europe following the Second World War; arranging transportation for nearly a million migrants during the 1950s. In 1975 IOM initiated resettlement programs for Indo-Chinese refugees and displaced persons and recently initiated the program in Thailand. I am ecstatic for this opportunity to be a part of their current mission.

We arrive at the airport and board a shuttle that transports us directly to an airplane parked a very long distance from the terminal. This airplane, a B-747, looks similar to others I have flown on but I do not recognize the airliner's name, "Flying Tigers", with an encircled "T" on the tail. Dr. Amos provides a short history: "At the end of WW2 a number of former American pilots formed the "Flying Tiger Line, an air freight company. In 1975 the Flying Tigers took part in relief efforts for Cambodians who were surrounded by Khmer Rouge forces. Dubbed "Rice Lift", it exposed the pilots to enormous risks when they delivered rice and other supplies under hostile conditions. Now they provide air transport for refugees re-settling in the U.S."

Within a short time, 130 Cambodians and Laotians join us in the Flying Tiger cabin. They are understandingly both excited and frightened at the same time; some are staring blankly around, others talking and giggling non-stop, while others, with tear-streaked faces, hesitate at the doorway and need urging to be seated. For almost all of our passengers, this is the first time they will fly. When several former KID refugees recognize me, they quickly walk to me, standing taller and smiling more broadly, with each step. Thirty of our passengers are under 18 years of age and only six or seven over 50 years of age.

Support staff, in addition to the IRC Team of 3 nurses and 3 doctors, from IOM and the airlines, totals 16 persons. The IOM staffers speak French and will be able to communicate in that language with most of our passengers. A few do speak some English. It takes a very long time to settle our passengers in their seats, and keep them there. They accept the unfamiliar packets of food but do not open them until re-assured there are more available. Beverages are drank copiously, only to be regurgitated later------

A Memoir—Delivering Health Care in Cambodian Refugee Camps, 1979–1980

We are finally airborne; I join the others in front row seats and we take turns sleeping. Our flight in this converted military transport is bumpy and ear-splitting noisy; keeping all of us busy with re-assurances that we are not crashing in the ocean. At least I pray we don't. At times, staff and passengers alike are nauseated and vomiting; overrunning the small bathrooms. The Asian custom of "squatting" rather than "sitting" on a commode, thereby creating constant movement of the commode seat, has resulted in the loss of the seats.

We are airborne for 24 hours; landing at the Anchorage, Alaska International Airport in the gloom of a frigid morning. This is a fueling stop only and neither the "Team" nor passengers are allowed to leave the airplane. Curiosity overwhelms them as many demand to have a "first peek" at this new country.

Bundled in blankets, several of the passengers take turns standing on the 5'X 5' square pad at the top of the steps, leading down to the ice-covered tarmac. Frozen dirty snow is piled against the buildings and a brisk wind is blowing. Thinking I could "memorialize this moment in time" with photos, I walk down the icy steps with my camera in hand, and promptly fall on my backside. I shoot photos until my film is out and run back up the steps to the relative warmth of the airplane. Only ten or so refugees braved the cold and warned the others "Stay inside. You will die in the refrigerator if you go outside." They thank me for my "bravery" and request photo copies. Only four photos turned out and I think my camera froze!

Back in the air, we fly six additional hours to finally land in L.A. Exhaustion, hunger and apprehension threaten to overcome me and I pray our entry will be problem-free. We stay close with our weary, silent passengers through Passport Control and Customs, encouraging and reassuring them. We are dismayed when Customs Officers confiscate small bags of rice and opium tucked into pockets and pant hems as our passengers had been thoroughly checked prior to leaving the Transit Centre. Our explanation of "rice symbolizing Good Luck and Prosperity in the new country" is accepted, and the rice returned. Our explanation of the use of opium in traditional medicine practices was not and the opium was not returned.

When we finally straggle through the Arrivals Door, we are greeted by a large Welcoming Committee with banners and music. Amid shy laughter, copious tears and many embraces, my "family" from KID is transferred to their sponsors. It has been over 36 hours since we left Bangkok; ten months since I left Montana. It feels like ten years---------I am numb with fatigue and time-lag, in need of a bath and real food, but I shoulder my backpack and search for a ticket counter. I have exactly 7 days to fly to Montana and return to Bangkok, if I wish to------Do I? It is too soon to tell.

Chapter 23

Montana Is My Home

It is surprisingly strange to be home again. Jet lag and exhaustion renders me numb and dumb. There hasn't been time or opportunity to notify my family or Marilyn, my house-sitter, of my flight from Bangkok so my unexpected appearance in my Helena home takes them by surprise.

I sleep for two days. I stumble up, eat, drink, and make telephone calls to my sons and my parents. They are speechless when I announce "Yes, I am back in Helena but only for a week. No, I am not sick. Yes, it good to have electricity and flush toilets and clean water. Yes, I promise to definitely return in time for Christmas." My beautiful and loving daughter, Laurie, drives over from Montana State University-Bozeman, to spend the week end with me. I touch and hug her constantly, wondering how I can leave her again. She admires my fit body and healthy tan; giggling when I tell her the attention my red hair and freckles brings me. I admire how my 'little girl' has grown into a self-assured young woman without me but irrationally feel hurt she did it on her own -- without me.

When I feel I'm adequately rested and fortified, I walk the two blocks to the Montana State Department of Health office to meet with Dr. Skinner, my Bureau Chief. I do not anticipate a warm welcome as he had approved a 90 day Leave of Absence and I am 240 days late in returning. Surprisingly, he shouts

"Welcome back" as I enter, grabbing me in a hug. He has never hugged me in the 5 1/2 years I have worked in this office. My co-workers enthusiastically hug me too, complimenting me on my changed appearance—thinner, younger, tanned and happier. My former secretary announces "We've having a welcome home party for you tonight at Rick's house so you can tell us about your adventures."

I must "talk" to Dr. Skinner - now. This "talk" does not go well. He grandly assures me, "You can return to your previous State Consultant's position in Disease Control. In recognition of your recent unusual experiences, you will be given more responsibilities. Unfortunately, due to your extended absence, your Merit Pay raises are forfeited. See you tonight!" He walks away before I can respond. Do I really want to return to this job, traveling and working long hours on less income? My State salary of $25,700.00 is barely enough to support me and keep my children in college; while I've almost doubled that amount in the past 6 months in Thailand. Hard, cold facts may help me make this decision as much as my personal desires.

Helena is beautiful any time of the year, but particularly in the autumn when the leaves are as golden and copper-hued as its history. The air is pungent with spruce and the surrounding mountain tops are dusted with snow. The odor of wood smoke is in the air as I walk the familiar steep path to Broadway and Last Chance Gulch; the site of the first gold mines. This small city was founded on those mines and copper ore and by cattle barons. My own 17 room home, built in 1868, is listed in the Montana Historical Register. Who wouldn't want to live in this unique place? 48 hours to departure----

Among familiar faces and familiar foods, my homecoming party makes me almost feel as if I had never left. At the same time I feel I am on the outside –looking in. Familiar party foods- homemade chili and breads, fresh, crisp green salads, and hot apple cobbler smothered in ice cream, smell and look delicious but I could eat little of the heavy and overly rich foods. My friends and colleagues, although excited to hear about my adventures in Thailand, are unable to relate to the horrors of the refugees' situation and are dismayed to hear of my living and working conditions. "How can you go back to that terrible place?" they ask. Tonight, I really need less criticism and more empathy. I need to hear that my return to Thailand is the right thing for me to do, not solely for the financial benefits but because what I contribute truly makes a difference in people's lives---39 hours to departure----

An often used Thai word, "mai pen rai", means "never mind" and is common for trivial events and major accidents alike. Reentry is the mental and physical phenomenon necessary for this farangi to adjust from the world of "mai pen rai" to this modern, faster-paced world.

The intensity of life for a farangi in a refugee setting is such that I have developed a mental set of two worlds. There is the world of comfort, status and conformity I am now in. Then there is the world of Khmers, pot-bellied, dying children, Thais, exotic foods, crowded days, short nights and distance artillery. The world I am returning to.

Sally Hilander, a friend and Staff Writer for the Helena Independent Record, requests an interview. She is aware of the Flying Tiger flights to transport refugees to the U.S; and informs me that the re-settlement programs are not well-received, especially the ones for Vietnamese refugees. Her two brothers fought in the Vietnam war. It is agreed, for her article, that the main purpose of my unexpected return was a "family emergency-my ill grandmother" and not to transport 150 more Asian refugees to the U.S.

I am not comfortable with this fallacy but have neither the time nor energy to debate the issues. Sally reminds me that I may be living and working here again and should be prepared for negativity in regards to my humanitarian work with the refugees. My own grandparents were German immigrants; my children's father's parents were Russian immigrants. We are a country of immigrants who have contributed much to make America so great. How can we deny these newest South-east Asian immigrants the same opportunities? And why would we when they have much to offer. I do not understand. ---24 hours to departure------

These final hours before departure are spent talking on the telephone to my Dad and my sons. They assume my "adventures" end when I return home in December, and my Dad sternly reminds me, "You are fortunate to have a government job that will reward you with a good pension in another 20 years." I shudder at the thought. My daughter has skipped several classes to spend our last hours together and drive me to the airport. I promise to return in 90 days or so--by Christmas. She promises to decorate the house, gather food supplies, and invite our family to welcome me home and celebrate the holidays.

Zero hours to departure. I am airborne. As the plane circles the verdant green valley and snow-topped mountains, I gaze down and silently pray I can keep my promise to Laurie and my family and return in December. The 28 hour flight will allow me uninterrupted time to reflect on the happenings of the past months. When I left this airport ten months ago, I had no inkling of the life-altering experiences awaiting me. Stamped in my memories are the unforgettable people, expatriates and refugees, with whom I have lived and worked with. Despite the stresses, disappointments, and occasional failures; the anticipation of my return to now familiar faces and places fills me with overwhelming joy.

Chapter 24

Return And Countdown To Departure

Thirty hours later I arrive in Bangkok's Don Muang Airport. Surprisingly, I feel re-energized as I am a much more seasoned traveler now than when I first arrived here 10 months ago. Passport Control and Customs procedures have become familiar and I have U.S. dollar bills ready to facilitate the process. The crowds, the heat and humidity, the pandemonium, the 'norm", for this airport, now seem "the norm" for me. I'm back. I expected to feel like I was "returning home", but I don't, and I don't understand why I don't.

I remain in Bangkok for several weeks to review my newly printed Public Health Nurses' Manual. It has turned out better than I expected and I appreciate World Concern's willingness to sponsor its production and distribution. My contract was generous. I agree to translations for Thai, French, and Cambodian language editions.

New volunteers for International Rescue (U.S.A.) and American Rescue Committee have arrived and our Agency Guest House is packed with the newcomers. Last November, when I first arrived with my CDC Team, we drove directly to the refugee camps due to the urgency of conditions. The new teams have the luxury to remain in Bangkok for two weeks of "orientation" and "acclimation". I suspect these are "code words" for shopping and sight-seeing and since I have not had that luxury of time to be a tourist I happily join them.

First is the boat trip down the Chao Phya River where we view Thai- style houses, ancient temples and breath-taking orchards and gardens. Thousands of Thais, in small wood and tin shanties, live out their lives on this river. Behind them we can see the opulent King's Palace. The next stop is the famous Golden Lord Buddha image, weighing 5.5 tons and covered in 18 K gold leaf.

The Snake Farm at the Pasteur Institute is where poisonous snakes are kept. The venom is extracted and taken to prepare vaccines which are distributed throughout the world. The process of milking the venom from the snakes is safe to watch but I am deathly afraid of snakes so keep a good distance between them and me.

A day trip to the Bridge on the River Kwai is of sentimental interest to those of us who remember World War II and the novel and movie that made it known. It was built to link Burma and Thailand but after 37 years remains unfinished. On the return trip we stop at a commercial crocodile farm and watch as expensive purses, belts and shoes are being hand-made. I like crocodiles just a tad less than the snakes---

My friend, Sheppy, at the U.S. Embassy, is on vacation so I am unable to visit with her. Dr. Rangaraj, my mentor, in the United Nations High Commission for Refugees Headquarters, is available. He arranges meetings with several officials in the U.N. departments, and lunch with heads of three Voluntary Agencies. I'm now certain I will not be returning to my Montana State Department position so must take advantage of my contacts while here. I leave with a packet of Letters of Recommendation attesting to my experience, expertise, and reliability.

Anything to do with refugees is about politics. These letters are a way to get my foot in the door of the many-roomed mansion of the United Nations. Once that blue globe adorns my resume, I will have gained a career, a lifetime badge of neutrality, and a universal entry into the wide world of humanitarian service. Thank you, Dr. Raj!

I make time to visit my favorite dress-makers and select designs and fabrics for my "Going Home Wardrobe." Lovely Thai silks and thin cottons will hardly be appropriate for winter in Montana but I am optimistic they will be needed on my next assignment. Wherever that is---

On my final night in Bangkok, I lead the newcomers to a now-established "initiation rite" in Soi Cowboy. Each visit to this street is like the first time-shocking, unbelievable fun. "Wanna dance with me! Wanna play with me!" "Come with me, I am #1 best!"

Returning to Aran is bittersweet. I surely didn't expect that there would not be any changes. I find a cot in Daniel's leased house but the new volunteers are strangers to me. Kid-I-Dang has taken on the appearance of an organized city. I am remembered and hear happy shouts of "Welcome back, Madame Chalot!" When I relate my Flying Tiger Adventure to America, they cry with happiness to know their friends are now safe.

There are Khmer-operated departments providing services to meet every need-health and medical, education, sanitation, food and water supplies, traditional music and dance shows, religious services, and the crematorium that was finally finished. The 75,000 refugees remaining here are still refugees with an uncertain future. Some have hope for re-settlement in another country and others may return to Cambodia under a U.N.-sponsored program. The adaptability of these tenacious people is admirable; reminding me of an ancient Chinese saying that advises "one to be like the willow tree and bend with the wind. Be not like the oak tree that will crack and fall down."

I re-visit Sa Kaeo Camp where I first landed 12 months ago but am unable to locate the original site of the Tri-age Unit where I started this journey. The dusty Camp is deserted as the last of the 3,000 Khmer Rouge refugees detained here have chosen to return to Cambodia. They were provided with rice seed to plant, farm implements and bus transportation across the Thai border to small villages. Their country is still at war and there are no guarantees they will not re-join the battle against the Viet Namese Army.

Suk Mai, although disappointed I am leaving Thailand, is still my "best friend." We make a final visit to the beauty parlor for special beauty treatments and body massage. My audience appears on schedule and admire my "red hair and freckled skin beauty". They are my friends, too, and this time I laugh with them.

Yat Nei is approved for third country re-settlement and will soon join her brother and family in the U.S. I give her my home address and telephone number and she promises to contact me when she is settled.

My final farewell party is somber. John and Daniel, Esmeralda and Barbara, Don and Phillip, Dieter and Paola---so many wonderful friends I would have never met if I had not come, and stayed. We traveled from many countries to do what we could to help in a desperate situation, because we cared. We have shared horrific tragedies with the dispirited refugees in our care, and, under our watch, many became survivors. I know that I am a much better person because of them, and because of the dedicated men and women I met and lived and worked and cried with. I'll always wonder if I have done enough. Could I have done more?

Daniel spoke for all of us when he said "I cry for all those people who have to carry on alone. I cry for the people blinded or crippled or orphaned or widowed-yesterday and tomorrow-by the land mines and the shelling, of not being able to have done more for those most dear to them, enduring torture that will not end. How can wounds like this ever heal? I want the world to cry again for the Cambodians, to cry and understand and feel, and hopefully to help-to help not only the Cambodian people but all people everywhere who have suffered and been displaced from their homes by famines and wars."

Perhaps, all the politicians who are the deciders; who authorize the bombing of innocent people who are not at war with us, should witness the results of their decisions. Perhaps, these politicians should be required to volunteer in a refugee camp, to witness the widows and the orphans despair. To feel the helplessness of the terrorized people who have had their lives and country taken from them by their decisions. Perhaps, then, they would work harder to create peaceful solutions to conflicts.

Now I return to my home in Montana, knowing I will not remain for very long. I realize that this unique experience will not be repeated in my lifetime but will become the springboard for my next assignments.

Farewell---sawadee---au revoir---auf weiderstein---ciao---shalom--my dear friends. May one day we meet again.

Chapter 25

Sa Wa Dee, Thailand-Shalom, Israel

It is time to return home. My dilemma lies in which direction should I travel to do that. Recalling my Israeli friend's invitation to visit Tel Aviv, I call Dr. Mick Alkan. He enthusiastically renews his invitation, promising to meet me on arrival with an itinerary for my ten day visit.

Before I can change my mind, I quickly confirm my pre-paid flight tickets on El-Al and British Airways to Tel Aviv via Cairo, Egypt. The bulging packet also contains my onward tickets from Tel Aviv to New York City, via Cairo and Rome. In New York, I plan to visit friends for three days before completing the final leg of my journey home-to Montana.

Fanning out my tickets on my narrow cot, I touch each one and feel my entire body tingle with anticipation. "What AM I doing?" I ask myself. Self answers, "You are living a dream. Remember the Bible stories you grew up with in the old Lutheran Church Sunday School? Travels in the Holy Land? Now you'll see Jerusalem and Bethlehem, and maybe even the Sea of Galilee!" Another adventure, of the many I've already experienced. Perhaps I should just go home.

During the long flight to Cairo, I read my Berlitz "Pocket Guide to Israel". It is surprising to learn that this country is only 260 miles long and 70 miles wide at its widest point. This is half the size of Montana! Tel Aviv is the first new Jewish city in over 2,000 years and I ponder the reasons for this.

I sleep through most of the flight but wake up when we land to refuel in the Cairo Airport. Passengers are not allowed to disembark during refueling stops so I can only gaze towards the air terminal in the hazy far distance.

Within a short time we are landing at Ben-Gurion Airport in Tel Aviv. Several hours pass while I trudge my way through a bewildering progression of Customs, Passport paperwork, and baggage searches. I answer repetitive questions on the purpose of my work and travels in Thailand. Security patrols, both armed and unarmed, are everywhere.

Finally, I am released to the Main Terminal Arrivals Lobby. I expect to be greeted by Dr. Alkan but am directed to a shuttle bus. Non-flight passengers are not allowed to in the terminal. The shuttle bus is only a 15 minute ride to the Airport Car Park where I am warmly greeted by Dr. Alkan and his family.

My first week is spent learning about life in the kibbutz. The family, which includes two sets of grandparents, have lived here for several years. Their homes are small and compact. With a great amount of time spent in communal activities outside the home, i.e. eating, working, attending classes and services, there is little need for larger living quarters. After my three days stay as a guest, I am required to contribute my "labor" to the commune's operations. My first "labor" is ladling homemade yogurt from huge aluminum vats into small serving dishes. All meals are eaten in a homey communal hall. My second contribution is assisting Dr. Alkan in the Children's Clinic. Here I feel more confident; administering immunizations to young children.

The kibbutz, surrounded with green trees and gardens, is also a farm with cows, sheep, chickens and goats. With the warm welcoming from the residents, I began to shed the tenseness I've felt for many months in Thailand. Perhaps I'll just stay here!

In this intriguing atmosphere, I am delighted to hear Michaela's children converse in Southern accented English. The family had lived in Tennessee for seven years while Michaela attended Vanderbilt University. The children acquired their English-speaking skills while growing up there.

BETHLEHEM

From the kibbutz, Mick and I drive to Jaffa, an ancient Arabian seaport and village on the Mediterranean Sea. We then drive on to Bethlehem, a Palestinian settlement where Christians worship in centuries old churches. We pass signs directing us to several "fields where the shepherds watched biblical flocks" and then I am left to wander on my own.

According to the Bible, Jesus was born in a stable in this small city. I visit the Milk Grotto and Rachel's Tomb and several other well-publicized sites before I decide there is simply an overabundance of history and tourists to absorb in a one day visit.

JERUSALEM

Mick has been unsuccessful in obtaining a permit for us to visit the Palestinian Sector, reported to be the largest refugee camp on earth. I am somewhat relieved to not have to witness more injustices to innocent children.

Instead we drive to the historic walled heart of Jerusalem, the Old City, which dates back to the time of Christ. Mick leaves me on my own to find a room in a small hostel near the Jaffa Gate, one of eight entrances that punctuate the ancient, towering city walls. I am overwhelmed with history. I spend one whole day simply sitting in the square, breathing in sights and sounds and exotic odors. Watching the vast array of people and cultures, reveling in the pandemonium of languages, I pinch myself to make certain I am not dreaming.

Joining a group of Christian pilgrims, I walk the Via Delorosa, (Street of Sorrows), following the final footsteps of Jesus as he made his way to Calvary. There are Fourteen Stations of the Cross. The marked points are under on-going dispute. A few are certainly the stuff of legend but the walk is impressive and informative. Food stalls along the way offer varieties of foods and I courageously sample many!

Back at the Jaffa Gate I find David Street which leads me to the legendary Western Wall, better known as the "Wailing Wall". From here I can see the Dome of the Rock, standing in the center of Temple Mount, whose golden cupola is the city's most famous landmark. My admission ticket allows me entry to the gold topped Dome built in A.D.688-691, and the nearby small Islamic museum.

My final day is spent sitting at a table in the sun. Drinking tiny cups of potent expresso, nibbling tidbits of unfamiliar but delicious foodstuffs. Watching the endless parade of multi-ethic people, and listening to the ebb and flow of multi-languages is exhilarating. I address dozens of holiday cards to my friends and relatives. The postage stamps are unique and the envelopes will be postmarked "Bethlehem." I even remember to address one to myself!

On my final evening in Israel, Danny, my moonlight dancing partner of Khao-I-Dang, collects me to spend an evening at his parent's home. His mother has prepared a special dinner for me and regardless of our language barriers (I speak no Hebrew and she little English), we enjoy each other's company.

When we return to the hostel, we find Mick waiting for us. We spend the remaining few hours of the night reminiscing our shared time and events in Thailand. My flight departs from Tel Aviv early so we start the drive before sunrise. We are now very quiet. We do not know what the future holds for me, or them and their families. With many hugs and kisses, we promise to stay in touch, no matter where in the world we may travel. Copious tears are shed as I board the airport shuttle that will take me to the Departure Gate. I can't look back. I am so glad I came and know in my heart I will someday return to this fascinating country.

Chapter 26

Coming Home- December, 1980

From the time I leave Thailand, I am consciously preparing myself for re-entry into my old, familiar world. The hectic, ten day stop-over in Israel with my former colleagues disrupted the process. My visit with old friends in New York City is designed to re-start the process, to re-acquaint me with our country's wealth and assumed security. No armed military waving guns, patrolled fences and constantly checked passes. No sick and starving children and forever lost families.

When I am sufficiently recovered from jet-lag and culture shock to venture out, my friends, previously from Montana, proudly introduce me to their adopted, beautiful city. The air is frigid and I shiver inside my borrowed coat and gloves. The spectacular Christmas decorations, the dazzling shops, the vast hordes of people and cacophony of traffic, are overwhelming. I am ready to journey on to serene Montana the following day. We had just entered a large, crowded café when everyone, inside and outside, stop talking and moving. The traffic has come to a complete halt. For a few moments, the silence is deafening.

It is December 8. The newscasters report that John Lennon, of Beatles fame, had just been shot and killed as he was standing in front of his apartment building. That building is within at least two miles of us. How can this terrible thing happen here? And why? From total silence to bombastic noise, strangers turn to each other and ask, "What happened? Why? Who was the shooter? Did he get away?" Our holiday spirits deflated, we return to my friends' home in silence.

The next day I depart New York City with great relief. I vow to never return.

Home for Christmas, as I had promised. As previously planned, my daughter had decorated our home for the holidays and there is an abundance of snow to add to the festive atmosphere. My parents and sister and family, my sons and their wives and children arrived laden with gifts and our favorite holiday foods. They politely look at my photos and listen to my descriptions of events but are visibly relieved when my dad firmly states "We have enough problems of our own here at home. We can't worry about what is happening to those people. Not our problem."

It was assumed I was returning to my Montana State position, and reluctant to disturb the holiday spirit, I didn't discuss details of my future plans.

Several churches and the local Kiwanis and Rotary Club chapters expressed interest in my refugee relief experiences, inviting me to speak and show my photos. My presentations were well attended although my audiences were more curious about me than the Cambodians tragic situation.

I was questioned about my motives for working in the refugee camps. The question was, "If you aren't a missionary, or sent by the government, and really too old to fit the "hippie" mold, why would you want to leave Montana?" I do not respond to these questions; sadly concluding my truthful explanations would not be understood.

I am proud to call Montana my home. A once popular song asks "How are you going to keep them on the farm, once they've seen Paree?" I haven't seen 'Paree' yet, but I intend to, and many, many more famous cities!

Postscript

After my return to Montana, Sally Hilander contacted me to provide current information on Laotian refugee re-settlement in Montana.

A little-known fact is that smoke jumpers from Montana were recruited by the CIA to work in Laos. Among those was Jerrold B. Daniels from Missoula, who in the early 1960's, became the liaison officer between General Vang Po and the CIA. For 20 years he worked closely with the Hmong, who were mountain villagers. When the communists took over Laos in 1975 and the United States pulled out, thousands of Hmong fled across the Mekong River to Thailand where they lived in refugee camps for many years.

Mr. Daniels remained in Southeast Asia until his death in 1982. As a chief Ethnics Affairs Officer in charge of the Highlander and Lao refugees, he helped his Hmong friends both in the camps and in resettlement in the United States. He facilitated General Vang Po, his family, and 2,000 Hmong villagers in their resettlement near Missoula, MT.

Mr. Daniels died at the age of 41 years at his home in Bangkok. His body was shipped back to Montana where Hmong friends and colleagues gathered from all over the United States to pay final tribute to their beloved friend at a traditional Hmong funeral ceremony.

ROTC Hall Of Fame-University Of New Hampshire And Air Force

COLONEL AMOS R. TOWNSEND, U.S.AIRFORCE, graduate of the University of New Hampshire and University of Pennsylvania. Studied biochemical warfare for the Air Force, and earned a Master's Degree in Public Health from Columbia University.

After interning at Andrews AFB,MD, he became a flight surgeon and was assigned to the 20th Tactical Fighter Wing at RAF Wethersfield, U.K. Colonel Townsend returned to work at the USAF Surgeon General's office from 1966-1969. He then volunteered for a two year tour at Pleiku and Phu Cat Air bases in South Vietnam. During that period, 1969-1971, he spent half of his time caring for indigenous Vietnam and Montagnard people, both military and civilian. Vietnam was followed by tours at U.S. air bases until he retired. In 1979, he again volunteered to work with Laotian, Vietnamese and Cambodian refugees in Thailand's refugee and displaced persons camps and holding centers.

REFUGEE SERVICES
Organizations

These voluntary agencies and international organizations provide refugee services in Thailand. Members of the CCSDPT are indicated with asterisks.

VOLUNTARY AGENCIES AND INTERNATIONAL ORGANIZATIONS

1*	ACEPT:	Ambassador College Educational Project in Thailand	23	HSF:	Holt Sahathai Foundation
2*	AFSC:	American Friend Service Committee	24*	ICA:	International Christian Aid
3*	AMG:	Advancing the Ministries of the Gospel	25	ICEM:	Intergovernmental Committee for European Migration
4*	AOG:	Assemblies of God Foundation	26*	ICMC:	International Catholic Migration Commission (Geneva)
5*	ARC:	American Refugee Committee			
6	AWC:	American Women's Club of Thailand	27	ICRC:	International Committee of The Red Cross
7*	BASE:	Belgium Aid to South-East Asia	28*	IMT:	International Medical Teams
8*	CAMA:	Cama Services, Inc.	29*	IRC:	International Rescue
9*	CARE:	Co-Operative for American Relief Everywhere, Inc.	30	JMT:	Japanese Medical Team
10	CBERS:	Community-Based Emergency Relief Services	31*	JVC:	Japanese Volunteer Center
11*	CCT:	Church of Christ in Thailand	33*	MCC:	Mennonite Central Committee
12*	CCU:	Church of Christ (Udorn)	34*	MHD:	Malteser-Hilfsdienst Auslandsdienst E.V.
13	CDC:	Center for Disease Control			
14*	COERR:	Catholic Office for Emergency Relief and Refugees	35	MIHV:	Minnesota International Health Volunteers
15*	CONCERN:		36		Monaco Medical Team: The Monaco Medical Team
16*	COR:	Christian Outreach			
17*	COSIGN:	Church of the Saviour International Good Neighbors	37*	MSF:	Medicins Sans Frontieres
18*	CRS:	Catholic Relief Services	38	NCA:	Norwegian Church Aid
19*	CUSO:	Canadian University Service	39	NRC:	Norwegian Refugee Council
20*	DPC:	The Displaced Persons Center	40*	OMF:	Overseas Missionary Fellowship
21*	FFFM:	Finnish Free Foreign Mission			
22*	FHI:	Food for the Hungry International	41*	OSB:	Overseas Service Bureau

continued

Map of Refugee Locations in Thailand - 2

MAP OF LOCATIONS OF CAMPS/HOLDING CENTERS/TRANSIT CENTERS IN THAILAND
(SITE, DISTRICT, PROVINCE)

		Camp Description
1.	Affected Thais, Thai-Cambodian Border	
2.	Aranyaprathet, Aranyaprathet, Prachinburi	C
3.	Ban Nam Yao, Pua, Nan	C
4.	Ban Vinai, Pak Chom, Loei	C
5.	Burirum, Muang, Burirum	C
6.	Chiang Kham, Chiang Kham, Phayao	C
7.	Ban Tong, Chiang Khong, Chiang Rai	C
8.	Kab Cherng, Kab Cherng, Surin	HC
9.	Kamput, Pong Nam Ron, Chantaburi	HC
10.	Khao I Daug, Ta Phraya, Prachinburi	HC
11.	Khao Larn, Muang, Trat	C
12.	Kho Prerd, Laem Singh, Chantaburi	C
13.	Lumpini Transit Center, Bangkok	TC
14.	Mairut, Klong Yai, Trat	HC
15.	Nong Chan, Ta Phraya, Prachinburi	BE
16.	Nong Khai, Nong Khai, Nong Khai	C
17.	Nong Samet, Ta Phraya, Prachinburi	BE
18.	Phanatnikhom, Phanatnikhom, Chonburi	HC, TC
19.	Lumpuk, Prasat, Surin	C
20.	Rangsit Transit Center, Bangkok (closed)	TC
21.	Ban Kaeng II, Sa Kaeo II, Prachinburi	HC
22.	Si khiu, Si khiu, Nakorn Ratchasima	C
23.	Sob Tuang, Mae Jarim, Nan	C
24.	Songkhla, Muang, Songkhla	C
25.	Suan Plu Transit Center, Bangkok	TC
26.	Ubon, Muang, Ubon Ratchathani	C

Index: BE - Border Encampment
        C - Camp
        HC - Holding Center
        TC - Transit Center
        Underlining - Refers to most common name.

continued

Refugee Services - 2

42	OXFAM:	Oxfam America	65	TRC:	Thai Red Cross Society
43*	RBT:	Redd Barna-Thailand	66	TRIP:	Thailand Refugee Instruction Program
44*	RCIR:	The Rescue Committee for Indochinese Refugees	67	UNHCR:	United Nations High Commissioner for Refugees
45*	Salvation Army:	The Salvation Army	68	UNICEF:	United Nations Children's Fund
46*	SAWS:	Seventh-Day Adventist World Service Inc.	69	USAID:	United States Agency for International Development
47*	SCF:	The Save the Children Fund	70	WFP:	World Food Programme
48*	SCF/USA:	Save the Children Federation USA	71	WICRR:	Wisconsin Indo-China Refugee Relief, Inc.
49	SDR:	Swiss Disaster Relief			
50*	SMP:	Samaritan's Purse	72*	WORLD CONCERN:	World Concern
51	Soforthilfe:	Soforthilfe			
52*	SPM:	Scandinavian Pentecostal Mission	73*	WRC:	World Relief Corporation
53*	SOS:	SOS/Enfants Sans Frontieres	74*	WRFF:	World Relief Friendship Foundation, Inc.
54*	TBM:	Thailand Baptist Mission			
55*	TBMF:	Thailand Baptist Missionary Fellowship	75*	WSUT:	Welfare Services Unit Thailand The Church of Jesus Christ of Later-Day Saints
56	TCP:	The Children's Project			
57	TCR:	Thai Committee for Refugee - Chao Surin Association - Barry Durance Foundation - Friends for All Children	76*	WVFT:	World Vision Foundation of Thailand
58	TCRS:	Thai/Chinese Refugee Service	77*	YMCA:	Young Men's Christian Association
59	TDF:	Tom Dooley Foundation	78*	YWCA:	Young Women's Christian Association
60*	TDH:	Tom Dooley Heritage, Inc.			
61	TDHG:	Terre des Hommes Germany	79*	YWAM:	Youth With A Mission Relief Services
62*	TEAR FUND:	The Evangelical Alliance Relief Fund			
63*	TOV:	The Ockenden Venture	80*	ZOA:	Zuid Ooste Azie
64	TPH:	Thai Public Health			

continued

CPSIA information can be obtained at www.ICGtesting.com
Printed in the USA
LVOW08s2016171014

409267LV00001B/7/P